Forty-Niner Fever!

by
Leonard Koppett

and

The Sports Staff of
The Peninsula Times Tribune

Book Design and Production by Publishing Services Center, Los Altos, California

Copyright © 1982 by The Peninsula Times Tribune, 245 Lytton Avenue, Palo Alto, California 94301.
All rights reserved.

ISBN 0-86576-044-6

First Printing, February 1982

Distributed by William Kaufmann, Inc., 95 First Street, Los Altos, CA 94022

Contents

Acknowledgments	iv
Walsh foreword	v
DeBartolo preface	vi
Koppett introduction	viii

Chapter 1	Triumph in Pontiac	1
Chapter 2	Joy in San Francisco	16
Chapter 3	Fifteen Days that Shook the Bay Area	26
Chapter 4	The Best Season	43
Chapter 5	The New 49ers	66
Chapter 6	Bill Walsh	79
Chapter 7	Joe Montana	94
Chapter 8	The Team by Units	102
Chapter 9	The Coaches	122
Chapter 10	And a Cast of Thousands	128
Chapter 11	The Super Bowl Game	138
Chapter 12	The 1981 Season Game by Game	155
Chapter 13	Records and Statistics	228
Chapter 14	History of the 49ers	239

Acknowledgment for contributions and cooperation that made this book possible is made to:

The Peninsula Times Tribune

Sports Staff

Bill Harke, editor
Rick Chandler
Danny DeFreitas
Kevin Doyle
Chuck Hildebrand
Larry Lavelle
Ken Luthy
Michelle Nolan
Dick O'Connor
Keith Peters
Ray Ratto
Paul Savoia
David Wik
Gene Williams

Others

David Burgin, editor
Mary Schmich
Joe Melena, photo editor
Bob Andres, photographer
Jean Dixon, photographer

San Francisco 49ers

Ken Flower
George Heddleston
Jerry Walker
Delia Newland

Also

Steve Daley, Chicago Tribune
The Associated Press
United Press International
The National Football League

Foreword

For a professional football coach, winning in the Super Bowl means reaching the goal towards which all that planning and effort, by an entire organization, is directed. For us in the 1981 season, it was all the more gratifying because we reached that goal even sooner than we had hoped.

But pursuit of that goal, whether it is actually reached or not, is a time-consuming process that requires great concentration from all involved. A football coach, during a season, has so much to do that deals directly with the next step, and the step after that, that there is little opportunity to enjoy triumphs, or dwell on defeats. Our attention must focus on what's to be done next.

Only after it's all over can one sit back and reflect and, if there has been success, truly enjoy it. This volume, therefore, is a welcome record of a memorable year, of special immediacy because it is the product of our local newspaper. The *Peninsula Times Tribune* serves Redwood City, where our training base is, and Menlo Park, where I live, and that gives this telling of our story a more personal touch.

Bill Walsh
Redwood City, Calif.

Preface

When I took charge of the San Francisco 49ers in 1977, I also took on two obligations. One was to see to it that this franchise, owned by a single family from its beginning and considered something very special by the people of San Francisco and the Bay Area, retained the special loyalty of its followers. Even though my home and other responsibilities were 2,000 miles away, my desire to become a part of what San Francisco treasured was strong at the start and grew stronger.

The other obligation was to produce the kind of winning team its fans deserved, an attractive team that could give them pleasure and pride.

I'm sure I didn't understand, at first, how much work and time it would take to live up to those obligations. That could be done only by gathering the right people with the right talents—coach, players, administrators, staff—and letting them exercise their talents. When I did understand how long a process that could be, I was willing to supply support, encouragement and patience for as long as necessary.

But I did understand, and share, from the very first day the eagerness of 49er fans for their share of victory. So the trip to the Super Bowl, sooner than we anticipated, meant most of all delivering to those fans (and to everyone in the Bay Area) the satisfaction they waited for through so many years. As thrilled and happy as I am for myself and for everyone connected directly with the 49ers, I am even more delighted for the fans and their community, and proud that the promise was made good.

This book, showing in such detail how it all came about, is a nice memento, but I hope it is also a suggestion: let's do it again.

Edward J. DeBartolo, Jr.
President.

Introduction

Reliving glorious moments is the essence of the pleasure sports fans get from America's most widely shared entertainment experience.

The San Francisco 49ers, in winning the National Football League championship on January 24, 1982, in Super Bowl XVI, completed a sequence of glorious moments that will remain legendary as long as major league sports are played. Just two years after posting the worst record in their league, they brought their home city its first championship ever after 36 years of yearning.

If you have any interest at all in the 49ers, this book will help you relive those six memorable months in which modest hopes blossomed into unsurpassable triumph. The story is retold in copious detail, with the immediacy of daily journalism, and with additional information you may not have come across before.

If you are not a 49er fan, this book will enable you to understand why those who are will never forget this season, and what they felt along the way.

Much of this material appeared originally in the *Peninsula Times Tribune,* the primary newspaper in the mid-Peninsula area south of San Francisco that includes Redwood City, where the 49ers have their permanent headquarters. It is, in effect, their hometown paper.

There is also new material, prepared especially for this book drawn from many sources, including official National Football League records. In particular, certain charts and tables have exclusive features.

These add up to the most complete and comprehensive account available of this remarkable event in the history of the National Football League, in the general history of the Bay Area, and in the permanent folklore of American sport. It serves as a record, a premanent reminder and an illumination of a rare and marvelous occurance, a "first time" that can never happen again.

It is organized, however in an unorthodox way. The separate sections are, to a large degree, self-contained. You can read the book from start to finish in the ordinary manner, or you can dip into sections of special interest in any order. The first part is the most general account of what happened; the second concentrates on the personalities and backgrounds of the people involved; and the final section provides detailed information that can be used for reference as well as for discovery, and will reward re-reading.

All of it is the collective work of the *Peninsula Times Tribune*'s staff, from the perspective of live reporting rather than historical research, closer in spirit to the instant replay than to some long-after-the-fact docudrama. *Forty-Niner Fever* may be a malady of indefinite duration, but this book is plainly labeled as a booster shot and not an antidote.

Leonard Koppett
for the sports staff of
The Peninsula Times Tribune.

To our colleagues, the sportswriters of America, and to the memory of Red Smith

Chapter 1

Triumph in Pontiac

On January 24, 1848, according to most encyclopedias, James Wilson Marshall discovered gold at Sutter's Mill, near Coloma. It took almost a year for the news to reach enough people to generate the California Gold Rush, so the thousands who finally poured into the Sacramento Valley in search of instant riches came to be known as the Forty-Niners.

Exactly 134 years later, to the day, the San Francisco 49ers struck football gold 2,000 miles to the east, in a Detroit suburb under a plastic roof during the coldest winter of the 20th Century. Their strike took the form of a 26-21 victory over the Cincinnati Bengals in Super Bowl XVI, the game for the championship of the National Football League and therefore, without argument, for the football championship of the world.

But it took no time at all for news of the modern 49ers to spread. In fact, from the very start of their operation and long before the final result was determined, their every move was being watched by 100 million observers. Word of the find at Sutter's

Mill had to be carried by horseback and a few primitive telegraph wires, and by mail on sailing ships. Pictures of every Super Bowl play were transmitted instantaneously by satellites in orbit and wires criss-crossing the earth.

Times had changed, but the co-incidence of dates underlined a similarity in public reaction to the two events: an urge to celebrate hysterically, to partake (even if indirectly) in the excitement, to believe that the new-found wealth would last forever.

Inside the Silverdome in Pontiac, Michigan, that fourth Sunday of 1982, the 49ers were completing an achievement every bit as unforeseen as Marshall's (which happened to fall on a Monday, by the way).*

Only 37 months before, in this very building, their franchise had hit bottom. In the final game of the 1978 season, with both regular quarterbacks injured, they had to use Freddie Solomon, a wide receiver who had not played quarterback since college. It was their 14th loss in 16 games and marked the end of the two-year reign of Joe Thomas. Thomas had come in as general manager when the DeBartolo family bought the team from the Morabito family.

A month later, Eddie DeBartolo Jr. made Bill Walsh coach and general manager, and a complete overhaul began. But the 1979 team, although it played better and regained some affection among

---

*In 1857, Marshall said he actually found gold "at half past seven o'clock on or about the 19th of January—I'm not quite certain to the day, but it was between the 18th and 20th of that month." But Jan. 24 is the day the sample was confirmed to be gold, at Sutter's Fort, and that's the official date.

its oldest supporters, also finished 2-14.

In 1980, a 6-10 record was considered a notable improvement, but perhaps the most painful loss of the season took place in the Silverdome: trailing 17-13 with 52 seconds to play and a fourth down on the Detroit 11-yard line, Charle Young worked himself completely free in the end zone—only to have Steve DeBerg throw the ball out of his reach.

And the Silverdome was also the site of the first game played by the 49ers in 1981, a season they approached with reasonable hope of winning half their games. Once again, the outcome was frustrating, a 24-17 loss in which Detroit scored 10 points in the last 28 seconds of the first half and the tie-breaking touchdown in the last 18 seconds of the game.

But that depressing start was followed by the amazing developments that brought the 49ers national attention, a 13-3 record that was the best in the league and the status of slight favorite in the Super Bowl. Now they were on a field where they had never won a game—a fact that wasn't publicized much, but well known to the older 49ers who had played through those bad years—going for the biggest prize this franchise had ever had an opportunity to win.

It started badly, as if there really were a Silverdome jinx at work. Amos Lawrence ran back the opening kickoff—and fumbled the ball into Cincinnati's possession on the San Francisco 26-yard line. The one thing that 49er planners wanted most to avoid—falling behind at the start—was about to happen.

Sure enough, in three plays the Bengals made two first downs and were on the San Francisco 5. But the 49ers stopped a running play, sacked the quarterback, forcing a third-down pass. Dwight Hicks intercepted this one and ran it out to the 32, and (as one commentator after another told his public) the bullet had been dodged.

From that point on, the 49ers dominated the first half. They marched in businesslike fashion 68 yards to a touchdown, scored by Joe Montana leaping over the line from one yard out. They stopped the next Cincinnati possession short of midfield, had to punt from their own end zone, and grudgingly gave ground until Cincinnati was in field-goal range. But when a pass was completed on the San Francisco 8, Eric Wright stripped the receiver of the ball and the 49ers recovered the fumble.

Whereupon Montana drove his team 92 yards—the longest sustained march in Super Bowl history—to a 14-0 lead.

Ray Wersching's bouncing kickoff made Cincinnati start on its 2, and after a punt the 49ers moved inexorably again from their own 34 to the Cincinnati 5, using up the closing minutes of the half. With 29 seconds left and only one yard needed for a first down, two passes failed so Ray Wersching kicked a field goal and it was 17-0 with only 18 seconds left.

But that was enough time to score again. This time the bouncing kickoff was fumbled by two Bengals and recovered by Milt McColl on the Cincinnati 4, so Wersching kicked another field goal and the lead became 20-0.

Whatever fans might have thought, or television executives feared, no one on either team doubted, at halftime, that the Bengals would strike back. The image of a wounded tiger being dangerous, corny as it might be, was simple football truth for a team of that quality in a championship game.

Cincinnati wasted no time driving 83 yards from the second-half kickoff for the touchdown that made it 20-7 and a competitive game. The Bengal defense sacked Montana on the first 49er play, on his 11, forced an exchange of punts, and drove from midfield to a first down on the San Francisco 3.

And that's where the sequence arose that will remain the most memorable feature of Super Bowl XVI, the goal-line stand that shifted the emotional momentum back to the 49ers. The first play gained two yards, but the next was stopped dead. A completed pass wound up a foot short of the goal line as Dan Bunz made a perfectly timed and perfectly aimed tackle of Charles Alexander. And on fourth down, the huge fullback, Pete Johnson, was piled up again.

However, there were still 16 minutes to play and the 49ers were pinned on their own 1-yard line. They kicked out across midfield, but the Bengals moved smartly to a touchdown in seven plays and it was 20-14 with 10 minutes to play. In practical terms, this wasn't very different from the situation that would have existed if the previous drive had scored. Psychologically it was very different indeed.

Nevertheless, the 49ers had to win the game now on offense. They could not afford to give Cincinnati the ball in good field position again, when one more touchdown could put the Bengals ahead. The 49ers had to, at the very least, move the ball and eat up time; and for any margin of safety, they had to score at least a field goal.

So they did exactly that. A pass to Mike Wilson, when it was second-and-15 on the San Francisco 22, gained to the 44 and put them into operating position for the first time in the second half. It was the last pass they had to throw. Using all running plays, they reached the Cincinnati 23 and with 5:25 to play. Wersching's third field goal made the score 23-14.

That meant Cincinnati would have to score twice to win but a touchdown and a field goal would do it, and there was plenty of time.

But Cincinnati's first play was a long pass—and Wright intercepted it near midfield. He ran it back to the Cincinnati 25 and made a mistake that might have won him permanent notoriety as a Super Bowl goat: he tried to throw a lateral. Fortunately for the 49ers, Willie Harper covered the ball on the Cincinnati 22, and the 49ers were in position for another field goal that would force Cincinnati to try for two touchdowns.

They got it, but not until they had eaten up another three minutes running the ball down to the Cincinnati 6. With a 26-14 lead, 1 minute and 57 seconds to play, and no time outs left for Cincinnati, they were completely in control.

Cincinnati, of course, would not stop trying and hoping. Six consecutive pass completions covered 89 yards and cut the margin to 26-21, but now there were only 16 seconds left. There was still a chance: an onside kick, a long pass, perhaps an interference penalty, and another touchdown were still possible. But the 49ers had Dwight Clark, their best pass receiver, properly placed to catch and hold the onside kick, and that was it. Montana knelt down with the ball for the one mandatory play, and the feat so unimaginable a few months ago had been accomplished. The 49ers were champions of the football world.

Then came the explanations.

Keena Turner missed one play, or maybe it was two. Nobody is quite sure even now, after the parade through downtown San Francisco feting the Super Bowl champions, how many plays the young linebacker watched when he should have participated. Even Chuck Studley, the 49ers' defensive coordinator and the man paid to punish such mental lapses, doesn't know what happened to Turner, or how long it happened.

"I can't tell you how many plays it was that we had 10 men on the field," Studley said with a bulb-nosed grin. "Not until I see the films, anyway, and that won't be for a long, long time."

The 49ers and Turner will have weeks before Studley gets back to film study. They all earned their rest by the victory over the Cincinnati Bengals for the right to call themselves professional football's best team, at least for a year.

The 49ers can say they are the best because, for one half and selected moments of a second, they were better than the Bengals. They were very much better for five plays and 5 yards in the third quarter, with control of the game on the line and their backs pushed squarely into their gaily painted end zone. Those five plays won the game for the 49ers. For want of 5 yards, the Bengals are second-best.

San Francisco entered the crucible called goal-line defense midway through the third quarter. The 49ers' 20-point first-half lead had shrunk by seven, and their dominance had shrunk into veritable atoms. The Bengals needed only 5 yards to reduce San Francisco's lead to 20–14, and had five plays to do it.

Eventually, the Bengals got their touchdown, but not then, at the time it could have done them the most good. They lost more than just the six minutes required to regain the ball and score. They lost their best chance to reak San Francisco's premature hold on the Vince Lombardi Trophy, the silver bauble that goes with the $32,000 each winning player receives for winning every playoff game.

Once, or was it twice, the Bengals failed to score against a 10-man defense? Turner was on the sidelines watching intently while Craig Puki, the linebacker who plays alongside him, waved frantically at the 49er bench.

"One of the coaches asked where I was, but it was too late," Turner said by way of explanation. "That happened to me two weeks ago, in the Dallas game. I think they scored on that one. We play so many goal-line defenses that I got confused. I couldn't hear the coaches say what defense they wanted, so I tried to look at the personnel going on the field."

As Turner said, too late. The one play he surely missed was a 2-yard gain by Cincinnati's Pete Johnson, a snowplow in fullback's clothing, that gave the Bengals a first down at the San Francisco 3-yard line. The one he might have missed was another 2-yard gain by Johnson to the 49er 1-yard line.

The next three plays will be remembered in story and song by 49er fans everywhere. All the failures of 35 seasons were avenged, with interest, by men named Reynolds, Bunz and Lott.

First, Reynolds. The Bengals used Johnson a third time, but Jack Reynolds met him at full burst for no gain. Reynolds, the 34-year-old 49er defensive guru, could see where the play was going because he had seen it so many times before. As he explained it simply, "I could just tell. They lined up that way. I just had that feeling for it, and that's how it happened."

The Bengals did not try Johnson again on third down from the 1. Instead, quarterback Ken Anderson faked a handoff to the bulky fullback and passed to his right to halfback Charles Alexander. He caught the ball turning back to his left and turned to step into the end zone. Instead, he turned into Dan Bunz.

"I knew he was close," the blocky 49er linebacker said. "I thought for a second to go for the interception, but I thought that might be too risky. What if I missed? So I just tried to tackle him."

Bunz drove Alexander back from the goal line about two feet, and down. Deception having failed, the Bengals went back to Johnson one last time. He never came close.

"He was following No. 40," Bunz said, referring to Alexander. "I think he ran into him. My job was to take the lead back, and when I hit him, I think Johnson ran into him."

As Bunz eliminated the blocking, Reynolds and Ronnie Lott collided with the faltering Johnson. To their right, 49er tackle Archie Reese lay on his back, kicking and pointing back toward the playing field in glee. Johnson had been stopped, and with him, the Bengals.

Lott jumped into someone's arms. Reynolds ran off the field and threw up. And Keena Turner smiled. His teammates' finest hour had bought all the 49ers Super Bowl rings with their stand, and less importantly, they bought him six months' grace from the accusing finger that is film study. It would be a nice flight home.

Ronnie Lott barely had enough time to unsquint his eyes from the onslaught of television lights when he heard the song.

"Stand up and fight," it went. "This is it."

Lott smiled, then let that smile grow into a grin. He stopped the next TV crew in its cable-clogged tracks and said, "Hey, I'll be back in a second. OK? I've got to be with my guys." He stood up and walked to a tight circle of fellow 49er rookie defensive backs, and he sang with Carlton Williamson, Eric Wright and Lynn Thomas.

"Stand up and fight, this is it," they crooned.

Kenny Loggins sings the song. The sentiment, however, belongs to all the San Francisco 49ers.

The 49ers won their first league championship in 36 seasons of trying with a kaleidoscopic mixture of muscle and trickery, dominance and submission, good luck and bad, resource and error.

Most of all, however, they won with perseverance. For a half, they made the Bengals rue the day they earned this rematch, taking a 20–0 halftime lead. For a quarter after that, the 49ers played as though their 21–3 victory in December was simply a cruel hoax perpetrated on their patient fans. And in the final period, the Niners simply did their duty, scoring just enough points at just the right times to keep the Bengals at arm's reach.

The first half began with San Francisco's only turnover of the game, a fumble on the opening kickoff by Amos Lawrence. It ended with the Bengals wondering how they played their way into a 20-point deficit. The answers were many and varied.

Lawrence's mistake, gathered in by Cincinnati's John Simmons at the San Francisco 26-yard line, was rectified minutes later when Dwight Hicks stepped in front of Bengal receiver Isaac Curtis for his 10th interception of the season.

The result was deflating to Cincinnati, which had hoped to get at least a field goal out of the turnover. The interception was far more uplifting to San Francisco. Quarterback Joe Montana, voted the game's most valuable player, engineered a smart 68-yard drive and capped it himself wth a 1-yard touchdown dive.

The most interesting thing about the march was the play of the offensive line. On several occasions, left tackle Dan Audick lined up outside right tackle Keith Fahnhorst to lead a phalanx of blockers on a march through the Bengals' left side. The result was several impressive gains running right by Earl Cooper and Bill Ring.

"I think we must have run that about 14 times," right guard Randy Cross said. "We did it a lot on the first drive and a couple of times on the second. Their guys must have felt like they were trapped on a little island all by themselves."

The second quarter produced an even greater feeling of isolation for the lads in the striped hats. A pass reception in front of the 49er goal line by Cincinnati media idol Cris Collinsworth became a fumble recovery for Thomas after Wright, who had been beaten on the play, knocked the ball out of Collinsworth's hands from behind. That play sparked the longest drive in Super Bowl history.

The Niners drove again late in the first half, marching from their own 34-yard line to the Cincinnati 5, before settling on Ray Wersching's 22-yard field goal with 15 seconds left. When Archie Griffin, Cincinnati's forgotten two-time Heisman Trophy winner, fumbled the ensuing kickoff into the hands of San Francisco's Milt McColl, the 49ers scored again. Wersching kicked a 26-yard field goal, 13 seconds after his first one, to give the 49ers their 20-point lead.

Both Griffin's fumble and Cincinnati's poor field position on the kickoff before that came as a result of line-drive kicks by Wersching. David Verser fumbled the first of the two ground balls and recovered just in time to be tackled at his 4-yard-line. For those efforts, plus his four field goals, Wersching won Cincinnati punter Pat McInally's MVP vote.

"Montana had a great game," McInally said. "But they don't give the field-goal kicker the MVP award. He was fantastic with his kickoffs and field goals. I never saw a kickoff performance dominate a game like his did."

Cincinnati scored to begin the second half, a 5-yard run by Anderson, who also threw for two scores on his way to a 25-for-34, 300-yard passing performance. Montana threw fewer balls, 22; completed fewer, 14; for fewer yards, 157, but he also threw no interceptions to Anderson's two. Montana's numbers were kept low, in part, by Cincinnati's blitz, which befuddled the 49ers through the third quarter. San Francisco ran only eight plays from scrimmage in the period for 3 yards. And all but one were runs.

"Why were we so conservative?" wide receiver Dwight Clark asked rhetorically. "It's called field position and them blitzing from everywhere. We had to be really conservative so we wouldn't get sacked, because we were so far in the hole to begin with."

Cincinnati could get only Anderson's touchdown out of the quarter, however, because the 49ers stopped the Bengals four times from inside the San Francisco 3-yard line late in the period. The Bengals drove 53 yards early in the fourth quarter to cut the 49er lead to 20–14, but their best opportunity had been wasted. The touchdown, a 4-yard pass from Anderson to tight end Dan Ross, enabled the Cincinnati receiver to set a Super Bowl record for catches with 11, good for 104 yards and two scores.

Inside the locker room, owner Eddie DeBartolo, Jr., staggered as he gloried in the victory. In one corner, California Governor Jerry Brown stood by himself looking very much like a foreigner waiting for a bus, and walking notepads, microphones and cameras searched earnestly for the faces and words that would explain San Francisco football's finest hour. The explanation came from a silver box the size of a backgammon case and it came from Ronnie Lott.

"I won the Rose Bowl and now this," he said. "Doing all these things is hard to realize. I was a bum at one time."

In the competitive sense, so were the 49ers. That's where the song comes in again.

"Stand up and fight. This is it."

On that subject . . .

. . . on the aborted Cincinnati drive

"If somebody were to tell me that they couldn't cross the goal line on four plays from the 3-yard line, I would have told them to go back to sleep. I mean, really, no way. But damned if we didn't do it. We only had 10 players on the field on the first play. Keena Turner (outside linebacker) wasn't in. I heard somebody yell 'Keena, Keena. Where the hell is Keena?' He got in for the second play. That was the greatest goal-line stand ever. It should go down in Super Bowl history."

—49er defensive tackle Lawrence Pillers

"I saw them raise up at the snap of the ball and I figured I could go under them. But they seemed to have everything closed up. They were in a gap defense called at the right time. It's tough to find a hole when there isn't one. There just wasn't anything there."
—**Bengal fullback Pete Johnson**

"It was a staff decision to go for the touchdown on the fourth down. We had run twice to the left and made nothing. Rather than run the same place three times, we felt we could go to the right. But they got good penetration. They made it tough for Pete to cut and find a seam. We have total confidence in that play. You don't run a play and say 'Well, I hope this one will work.' We knew it would work because it had worked all season."
—**Cincinnati offensive coordinator Lindy Infante**

. . . on losing in the Super Bowl

"I came in at halftime and what I saw was a room full of men with their heads down. I said, 'Boys, it's about time we caught a kickoff. It's a damn shame to play like we have all year and then go out and embarrass ourselves.' They came back and fought the good fight, to the end. Nobody chucked it in. If you want to find me crying, you've come to the wrong man. Nobody expected us to even win our division. We weren't even picked for third. We had a hell of a year."
—**Bengal head coach Forrest Gregg**

"It could have been the greatest comeback in the history of the Super Bowl. It's too bad we just stood around and watched the first half go by. We're proud of how far we came in 1981. Look around this locker room at these guys. In the second half we came back. If we could have had a break in the fourth quarter, we might have made it back."
—**Cincinnati wide receiver Cris Collinsworth**

Chapter 2

Joy in San Francisco

The celebrating began immediately. David Burgin, editor of the *Peninsula Times Tribune,* is no stranger to the San Francisco sports scene, having once been the sports editor of the *San Francisco Examiner*. He was an eyewitness to the joy that erupted there as the game ended, and late that night, back in Palo Alto, wrote this account of it:

SAN FRANCISCO—There isn't a city in the world that knows how to party like San Francisco. In the precision of the idiom, they went nuts here Sunday evening and well into the wee hours.

If you were there, you know. I was there, and I've never seen, heard of or read about anything quite like it.

My companion said, "Geez, can you believe this madness? You'd think we had won a war."

It was better than that, in the sense that war is horrible. This was revelry over a football game, a season of games, and nothing more serious.

Here was the celebration of a team, the San Francisco 49ers, who realized a dream thought impossible by even their most faithful followers.

A brilliantly performed, six-month drama ended Sunday as the 49ers actually went to the Super Bowl and then won the darn thing, played in a depressed refrigerator of a spot called Pontiac, Michigan by defeating the Cincinnati Bengals, 26–21, for the championship of the National Football League.

I will not attempt to give it any more meaning than that. As for the ensuing celebration in the streets of San Francisco, down on the Peninsula or wherever in the Bay Area, about the only thing that made any sense was the senselessness of unbridled joy.

For my part, I drove around the city for an hour or so to see what it was like and I honked my horn along with everyone else. I couldn't stop laughing. Every sight and sound brought a giggle. I've never seen a throng so happy or a mood so infectious.

"Forty-Niner-Fever" was real.

On Union Street I rolled down my window and stuck my hand into that special San Francisco chill—somebody on the radio said the temperature was in fact 49 degrees—and exchanged a high-five and a soul-slap with a guy hanging out the back of a pickup truck traveling in the opposite direction.

At a red light on Franklin Street, the doors of the Datsun in front of us were flung open and out poured what seemed to be a dozen persons. As if they had rehearsed for a circus act, they did a bunny hop around their car in one direction, reversed it, then piled back in just as the light changed.

At practically every corner kids had shinnied up light poles and held signs or hollered, "We're

Number One."

Anyone who owned a trumpet took it into the streets, it seemed.

Perfect strangers, all ages, hugged each other and danced.

I saw a pretty woman of perhaps 20 plant a beauty flush on the lips of a handsome man of perhaps 70. No harm, no foul.

At the corner of Union and Laguna, a woman well beyond her college days stood atop a city trash can and did the Twist. Or something.

People were passing beer from car to car. We could have had at least a free six-pack, but I had to drive back down 101 and it would be my luck to get nailed by a CHP officer who happened to be an Oakland Raider fan.

Later I heard on the news that as the booze flowed and as the celebration became too much for a few, there were some injuries and arrests and a couple of dangerous bonfires set. All I saw was happiness.

I watched the game with about 20 friends at the Twin Peaks home of Carla and Hank Greenwald. I got there right at the opening kickoff and rushed in just as "Famous" Amos Lawrence fumbled and turned the ball over to the Bengals.

"Oh, no," I moaned. "The worst start imaginable."

"I don't know," Hank Greenwald, the sportscaster, said, deadpan. "Pearl Harbor was worse. And we came back from that one."

At the end of the three hours of cheering and analyzing, we sipped good champagne and Hank gave a toast. "This is to those of us who thought we'd never live to see the day the 49ers would win the Super Bowl," he said.

From the Greenwald's back porch you could hear the party starting in the city—fireworks, horns, hollering. Carla Greenwald had decorated their living room in 49er colors. A vase of gold and red carnations atop the TV set caught the last rays of a buttery sun dipping into the Pacific. I have no idea what that means.

Driving down into the city, we rounded a bend on Portola and there was the San Francisco panorama, twinkling as I'd never seen it. It will twinkle again tonight, after today's parade to welcome masterful coach Bill Walsh and his marvelous staff and team. It will bask and twinkle for many days to come, I'm sure.

And down the Peninsula

The screams of "We're No. 1" intensified with 14 seconds remaining in Super Bowl XVI Sunday.

Dwight Clark had just tucked in an onside kick to preserve San Francisco's 26–21 victory over Cincinnati in Pontiac, Mich., and assure 49er fans in the Bay Area that their team is, indeed, No. 1 in the National Football League.

A wild celebration, New Year's Eve and much more all over again, then followed in the Bay Area.

Peninsula streets, especially El Camino Real, deserted during the game as people were glued to television sets, became crowded with fans screaming and dancing. Firecrackers went off. Champagne corks were popped. Kisses and hugs were exchanged.

Few cars went by without a honk of the horn. Fans leaned out their car windows, wearing and waving red and gold, the 49ers' colors.

It was one big party and nobody had to be invited.

There were, however, a few minor fender-benders among the parading four-wheel vehicles. But the victims didn't even seem too upset. After all, the 49ers were Number One.

Finally, after 36 years, the 49ers had won their first championship of any kind for a San Francisco team.

Fans began to crowd bars Sunday night, not a normal night for big business. Most bars broke attendance records.

One of those bars was Bourbon Street at the Old Mill shopping complex in Mountain View.

Many fans at Bourbon Street had watched the entire game there. They felt it was the next best place to be besides Pontiac.

"I've caught 49er fever and I wanted to be with a big crowd," Taylor Barcroft of Palo Alto said.

Bourbon Street was one of several Peninsula bars that showed Super Bowl XVI on a big screen. There also were three other television sets in Bourbon Street as nearly 350 people watched.

A treat for late-comers to Bourbon Street was a recording of the entire game. By 8 p.m., the game already was on its third showing. An employee said it would be shown all night. The celebration continued until 1:30 a.m.

"I like the replay, because I know when all the big plays are coming," Barcroft said. "I've been watching the first half, then dancing during the third quarter when the Bengals dominated. I'm glad they taped it. I couldn't see it that well live because I was sitting in the back. I came early (10:45 a.m.), but I still couldn't get a good seat."

Rudy Santellan of Mountain View went to Bourbon Street in the evening because he knew the game would be replayed.

"I couldn't miss a second chance," said Santellan, as the crowd was cheering Cris Collinsworth's second-quarter fumble. "It was the best game ever in all of sports. Even better than the United States' Olympic hockey team victories."

Most of the crowd felt it was the best Super Bowl game ever.

The 49ers' Super Bowl victory seems to have brought people in the Bay Area together.

"I've never spoken to strangers as much as I have today," Elizabeth Burke of Los Altos said. "Everybody is going out of their way to smile at one another."

Cathy Dunsmore of Palo Alto agreed. "All of a sudden everybody loves everyone else."

Bill Anderson of Santa Clara, an employee at Bourbon Street, said he probably won't see another crowd as big as Sunday's until the 49ers make it into next year's Super Bowl.

On Monday, a parade through the center of San Francisco to City Hall brought out crowds estimated at 500,000—in a city whose official population is 679,000. The 49er players and officials,

49ers at San Francisco Civic Center

whose charter flight back from Detroit that morning was directed to a secret and secured landing area at the airport, rode on motorized cable cars. The crush was so great that police rerouted the procession from Market Street to Howard Street for several blocks—provoking a storm of subsequent complaints from celebrants who spent hours standing at what were supposed to be vantage points and wound up seeing nothing.

By Tuesday, the six 49er players who had been chosen by their peers to play in the Pro Bowl were in Hawaii, a day behind the other All-Stars reporting for the January 31 game. One of them was

Randy Cross, an outstanding offensive guard for several seasons only now getting full recognition, who also displayed a hitherto hidden talent for the witty and cutting remark. Upon reaching the snowbound Detroit area, he had declared, "going to the Super Bowl here is like having your parents promise for years to take you to Disneyland, and then winding up at Frontier Village."

After the game, he had told Paul Zimmerman of *Sports Illustrated* that he didn't mind missing that first Monday night meeting in Hawaii of the all-star team being coached by John McKay of Tampa Bay. To a UCLA alumnus like Cross, McKay is still more strongly identified as the former USC coach.

"It's only McKay's offense anyway," said Cross, with his deadpan delivery that enhances the joke and gets him into trouble. "If guys from USC can learn it, how complicated can it be?"

The intensity of the celebration got nationwide attention. *The New York Times* quoted a San Franciscan who said, "This is God's way of making it up to us for the 1906 earthquake."

What triggered so cosmic a reaction? After all, only one year before the football fans of the same area had enjoyed an equally dramatic, and equally unexpected, Super Bowl triumph scored by the Oakland Raiders. Yet that was greeted by just ordinary glee.

The biggest difference, naturally, was the identification "San Francisco," which meant different things to different people than the identification "Oakland." World championships had come to teams based in Oakland in baseball, football and basketball, but never before to a team carrying the San Francisco name. And the 49ers, created in 1946, were the first major-league team of any kind to represent San Francisco, so that deeper proprietary feelings were attached to them than to later arrivals.

The 36 years San Franciscans had to wait for this first championship had been exceeded only once in pro football history. Rooters of the Pittsburgh Steelers had to wait 41 years, from the team's inception to its first title in the 1974 season.

In 36 years, pent-up emotions can get pretty pent up, even if many of the present revelers hadn't been aware of feeling frustrated until the winning season reminded them that they were supposed to be.

In two respects, however, the 49ers had made some indelible history. They were the first team ever to win the Super Bowl the year after a losing season, and only the fourth professional football team ever to win as many as 16 games in one season. And those were universal, not just parochial, distinctions.

The Only 16-Game Winners in Pro Football History

Season	Team	Coach	Record (including playoffs)
1972	Miami Dolphins	Don Shula	17-0
1978	Pittsburgh Steelers	Chuck Noll	17-2
1976	Oakland Raiders	John Madden	16-1
1981	San Francisco 49ers	Bill Walsh	16-3

Chapter 3

Fifteen Days that Shook the Bay Area

The Super Bowl weekend hysteria did not arise in a vacuum. It came as the climax of two weeks of mounting monomania, triggered by a 28-27 victory over the Dallas Cowboys in the National Conference championship game at Candlestick Park on January 10.

Until then, even though the 49ers had finished first in their division, had scored notable regular-season victories over arch-rival Los Angeles, had won impressively at Pittsburgh and at Cincinnati, had routed the Cowboys 45-14, and had beaten the New York Giants in their first playoff game, they were still only football news. They didn't become a cultural phenomenon, and a national television attraction, until the playoff with Dallas.

There were three good reasons for this effect.

One was the long-familiar designation of Dallas as "America's Team," an open invitation to attach special significance to any victory over the Cowboys by any rival.

Another was the specific history of the Dallas-San Francisco series. Only three previous 49er teams, in 1970, 1971 and 1972, had ever reached the National Football League playoffs. Each was then eliminated by Dallas, twice in the semi-final round and, in 1972, in the first round in excruciating circumstances. That was the game in which the 49ers had a 28-13 lead in the fourth quarter and a 28-16 lead with two minutes to go, only to have Roger Staubach engineer a 30-28 Dallas victory with two touchdown passes connected by a successful onside kick.

Then there was the January 10 game itself, full of spectacular plays, see-saw scoring and a melodramatic happy ending.

The touchdown that made the score 27-27 with 51 seconds to play, and enabled Ray Wersching to kick the winning point, came on a sensational leaping catch by Dwight Clark at the back of the end zone of an off-balance pass by Joe Montana. Then, with one long pass after the kickoff, the Cowboys moved to the brink of field-goal range before the 49er defense created a sack and a fumble that ended the threat. (If Dallas had won again by the same 30-28 score so many fans remembered, there's no telling what sort of mass depression might have afflicted the San Francisco psyche.)

From the moment of "the catch" (captured magnificently by still photographers as well as reshown countless times on television), the 49ers were a phenomenon rather than just a football team.

For the next 15 days, there was no challenge whatever to the status of the 49ers as "Topic A" in the Bay Area news media. The rest of the universe, no doubt, continued to exist, but it was strictly in second place.

Everything considered, the Dallas game was the "best" football game ever played in San Francisco (in terms of its impact and outcome), and people simply couldn't read enough about it. Nor could they separate it from the dazzling thought, "we're going to the Super Bowl!" In Ray Ratto's column in the *Peninsula Times Tribune*, the immediate response was described this way:

Dwight Clark wasn't sure he could catch the ball Joe Montana threw. The pass looked high, too high.

"I was thinking, 'I don't know if I can get that,'" Clark said. "And right when I caught it, I thought, 'You almost jumped too soon.' I sort of caught it twice; it hit one hand, then the other."

Everson Walls was about three yards to Clark's right when the ball arrived. He watched Clark's jump, saw him land with the ball and turned his face away. He said two words: "Oh, no."

Oh, yes. The San Francisco 49ers are going to the Super Bowl. Clark's catch, a modest six-yard touchdown reception with 51 seconds remaining in Sunday's NFC championship game with the Dallas Cowboys, won for the 49ers a trip to the most important game of their lives, and of their fans.

True believers knew the 49ers would win as soon as they took the ball at their own 11-yard line. The Niners were being asked by their coach, the soon-to-be-canonized Bill Walsh, to cover 89 yards in four minutes and fifty-four seconds against one of the best defensive teams in the National Football League.

Keith Fahnhorst was one of those who believed. The bulky tackle who battled valiantly to earn a draw with Dallas' routinely brilliant defensive end, Ed "Too Tall" Jones, smiled when he was asked to remember those four minutes.

"I had complete confidence," the 49er with the second-most seniority said. "It sounds phony, but I had the feeling when we got the ball at the 11. I had no doubt at all. Destiny? God, it sure seems that way."

The drive was truly memorable, even more so than the one that beat the Los Angeles Rams in late November. Then, the 49ers had to cover 61 yards in less than two minutes just for a field goal that would clinch the Western Division of the National Conference. That was when the division title meant something. Today, it is extremely small potatoes, indeed.

Sunday, they had to march 89 yards in twice the time, but didn't have the luxury of settling for three points. They had to score a touchdown or be deprived, of a trip to the ultimate football game.

The stars of the drive were an odd blend of the already famous and the almost anonymous. Running back Lenvil Elliott, a forgotten old warhorse called back into service when Paul Hofer blew out his knee for perhaps the last time, ran around the weary Cowboy ends to get the 49ers out of the shadow of their own goal posts. Wide receiver Freddie Solomon reversed for 14 yards on a stunning bit of Walshian deception, and later caught a pass to move the 49ers to the Dallas 13-yard line. Montana, the alternately boyish and cold-blooded quarterback of three years' experience, ran the drive with the steely precision now expected of him on every 49er possession.

And there was Clark. Earlier, the 49er wide receiver had caught a 10-yard pass along the right sideline from Montana to move the 49ers to the Dallas 25, and now he was being asked on third down and three yards to go from the 6-yard line to run a pattern that had produced a touchdown for Solomon in the first quarter.

"It's called a sprint right option," Clark said, staring glassy-eyed into space. "The option is, Joe can throw to me or Freddie, or he can run it. Basically, I line up about six yards outside the right tackle and Freddie is three yards inside me. I go inside and look back to see which way Joe is rolling, and then I go that way."

He said all this while trying vainly to suppress a hacking cough, a remnant of his midweek bout with the flu, which is still leading Clark on points going into the late rounds. He looked peaked, and someone asked him how he could have freed himself of the pesky Walls, the Dallas defender who already had intercepted two passes and recovered a fumble, and still had enough strength left to leap for Montana's pass.

"How does the lady pick her car up off the baby?" he answered. "It was something we had to do."

Six lockers away from Clark, Fahnhorst lunged over a couple of reporters and grabbed Hofer, who wore street clothes and a grin barely confined by his ears.

"Come here, scum puppy," Fahnhorst yelled. They hugged, and then were joined by O.J. Simpson, another 49er in spirit and street clothes, for the greatest moment in the franchise's history. Fahnhorst, too, had been sick through the week and did not practice Tuesday, Wednesday or Thursday. He was needed to block Too Tall Jones Sunday, however, and couldn't take the day off no matter how sick.

"I was a little tired out there in the fourth quarter," he said, "but the adrenalin gets to flowing in that last drive. Right now, I could throw up on you, but when you're out there you just want to play.

"I remember the catch. I saw two guys coming toward my feet. I went down and then I looked up and saw (Clark) catch the ball. I wanted to go congratulate him, but I was paralyzed. It's all a blur even now."

No it isn't. The San Francisco 49ers are going to the Super Bowl. If Dwight Clark didn't know he could catch that ball before, he knows now. And he, like anyone who ever admitted to being a 49er fan, will never ever forget.

Play-by-play of NFC championship game

First quarter
(Time left to play in parenthesis):
Wersching kicked off out of bounds, for a 5-yard penalty.
Newsome returned Wersching's kickoff 19 yards from the Dallas 7.
Dallas ball, 1/10, on D 26.
Dorsett gained 2, sweeping right.
White's pass incomplete.
White was sacked by Board for loss of 11.
White's 49-yard punt was returned 3 yards by Solomon.
> San Francisco ball, 1/10, on SF 37 (13:12).
> Montana passed to Shumann for 11 and a first down on SF 48.
> Montana's pass incomplete.
> Cooper gained 3 on a pitchout to the left.
> Montana passed to Young for 17 and a first down on D 32.
> Montana passed to Elliott for 24 and a first down on D 8.
> Montana passed to Solomon for 8 and touchdown.
> Wersching's conversion made score San Francisco 7, Dallas 0 (10:41).

Jones returned Wersching's kickoff 18 yards from the D 11.
Dallas ball, 1/10, on D 29.
White passed to DuPree for 5.
Dorsett gained 8 up the middle for a first down on D 42.
Dallas penalized 10 yards for holding on White's incomplete pass.
Dorsett gained 5 on draw.
Dorsett gained 9, sweeping right.
White passed to Johnson for 20 for a first down on SF 34.
Jones lost 2, stopped by Reese.
Jones gained 6 on draw.
White passed to Jones for 3.
Septien's 44-yard field goal made score San Francisco 7, Dallas 3 (4:44).
> Ring returned Septien's kickoff 17 yards from the SF 4.
> San Francisco ball, 1/10, on SF 21.
> Montana passed to Young for 8.
> Montana's pass incomplete.
> Ring fumbled, Hegman recovering for Dallas.

Dallas ball, 1/10, on SF 29 (3:39).
Jones gained 3.
White passed to Hill for 26 and touchdown.
Septien's conversion made score Dallas 10, San Francisco 7 (2:49).
> Lawrence returned Septien's end-zone kickoff to the SF 17, and SF was penalized 8 yards for an illegal block.
> San Francisco ball, 1/10, on SF 9.
> Elliott lost 3, sweeping right.
> Cooper gained 6, up the middle.

[31]

Montana's pass incomplete.
Miller's 37-yard punt was returned 13 by Jones.
Dallas ball, 1/10, on SF 36 (1:33).
White's pass incomplete.
White's screen pass to Springs lost 3 on tackle by Harper.
White passed to Conley for 4 as quarter ended.

Second quarter
Dallas ball, fourth and 9, on SF 35.
White punted into the end zone for a touchback.
San Francisco ball, 1/10, on SF 20 (14:52).
Cooper lost 2, sweeping left, tackled by Martin.
Ring gained 11, sweeping right.
Montana passed to Young for 4 and a first down on SF 33.
Cooper gained 2.
Montana passed to Clark for 38 yards and a first down on D 27.
San Francisco took its first timeout.
Montana was sacked by Martin for loss of 11.
Montana passed to Clark for 10.
Montana's pass, for Wilson, was intercepted by Walls on the D 2.
Dallas ball, 1/10, on D 2 (9:57).
White had no gain on sneak.
Springs gained 1, up the middle.
Jones gained 7, sweeping right.
White's 37-yard punt was taken by Hicks on a fair catch.
San Francisco ball, 1/10, on D 47 (8:19).
Cooper gained 11, up the middle for a first down on the D 36.
Montana passed to Solomon for 12, for a first down on the D 24.
Elliott gained 4.
Montana, under pressure, passed to Clark for 20 and a touchdown.
Wersching's conversion made the score San Francisco 14, Dallas 10 (6:12).
Jones returned Wersching's kickoff 20 yards from the goal line.
Dallas ball, 1/10, on D 20.
Springs gained 3.
Dorsett gained 6.
White passed to DuPree for 3 and a first down on D 32.
Dorsett gained 4 on pitchout to right.
White passed to Hill for 17 and a first down on SF 47.
Lott's interception of White's pass for Pearson was nullified by a pass interference penalty for a first down on SF 12. (Lott had returned it to SF 37).
Dorsett gained 5, up the middle.
Springs gained 2.
Dorsett gained 5, sweeping left, for a touchdown.
Septien's conversion made score Dallas 17, San Francisco 14 (2:30).
Lawrence fumbled. Ring returned Septien's kickoff 14 yards to SF 20.
San Francisco ball, 1/10, on SF 10.
Montana's pass incomplete.

Elliott gained 3, sweeping left.
Two-minute warning.
Montana was sacked by Jones for loss of 8.
Dallas took its first timeout (1:55).
Miller's 37-yard punt was fumbled by Jones and recovered by Lawrence for
San Francisco on the Dallas 42.
San Francisco ball, 1/10, on D 42 (1:45).
Dallas was penalized 5 yards for defensive holding.
Cooper gained 5, but Clark was penalized 15 yards for illegal block, to D 45.
Montana was sacked by Martin for loss of 7 and fumbled,
Bethea recovering.
Dallas ball, 1/10, on SF 48 (1:24).
White was sacked by Stuckey for loss of 7.
White's screen pass incomplete.
White sacked by Pillers for loss of 13. White fumbled and recovered.
San Francisco took its second timeout (0:44).
White's 40-yard punt was returned 9 yards by Hicks.
San Francisco ball, 1/10, on SF 37 (0:34).
Montana passed to Clark for 7.
Montana passed to Clark for 11 and a first down on D 45.
San Francisco took its third timeout (0:11).
Montana passed to Solomon for 16 and a first down on D 29, as half ended.

Third quarter

Lawrence returned Septien's kickoff 24 yards from the SF 1.
San Francisco ball, 1/10, on SF 25.
Elliott gained 5.
Cooper gained 3.
Ring was stopped for no gain by Jones and Bruenig.
Miller's 33-yard punt was fumbled and recovered by Jones.
Dallas ball, 1/10, on D 34 (12:56).
Dorsett gained 5, sweeping right.
Dorsett gained 1.
White, chased by Board and Harty, was penalized 17 yards for intentionally
grounding a pass.
White's 39-yard punt was returned 12 by Hicks.
San Francisco ball, 1/10, on 50 (11:07).
Montana's long pass incomplete.
Ring gained 9 up the middle.
Montana gained 2 for a first down on D 39.
San Francisco was penalized 10 yards for holding (Montana's pass
incomplete).
Montana passed to Young for 16.
Montana passed to Cooper for 6, for a first down on D 27.
Elliott gained 4.
Cooper gained 7, up the middle, for a first down on D 16.
Montana's pass off Elliott's hands was intercepted by R. White.

Dallas ball, 1/10, on D 13 (7:41).
White's pass incomplete.
White's pass off Spring's hands was intercepted by Leopold on D 18 and returned 5.
> San Francisco ball, 1/10, on D 13 (7:25).
> Ring gained 6.
> Easley gained 2.
> Dallas took its first timeout.
> Ring gained 1.
> On fourth and 1, Montana gained 1, but Dallas offside. The half-the-distance penalty gave San Francisco a first down on D 2.
> Davis hit the middle for 2 and a touchdown.
> Wersching's conversion made score San Francisco 21, Dallas 17 (5:44).

Wersching kicked off out of bounds, for a 5-yard penalty.
Jones returned Wersching's kickoff 18 yards from the Dallas 13.
Dallas ball, 1/10, on D 31.
Dorsett gained 2.
Dorsett gained 2 on pitchout left.
White passed to Jones for 10 and a first down on D 45.
Dorsett gained 7, up the middle.
Springs gained 3, for a first down on SF 45.
White passed to Springs for 4.
Dorsett gained 1.
A 28-yard pass interference penalty on Lott, covering Johnson, gave Dallas a first down on SF 12.
Dorsett was stopped for no gain by Reese, as third quarter ended.

Fourth quarter

Dallas ball, second down and 10, on San Francisco 12.
White passed to DuPree for 7.
White's pass for Crosbie in end zone broken up by Wright.
Septien's 22-yard field goal made score San Francisco 21, Dallas 20 (14:08).
> Lawrence returned Septien's kickoff 17 yards from the San Francisco 2.
> San Francisco ball, 1/10, on SF 19.
> Montana's long pass incomplete.
> Montana passed to Solomon for 21 and a first down on SF 40.
> Elliott gained 4, sweeping left.
> Easley gained 4 and fumbled, Walls recovering for Dallas.

Dallas ball, 1/10, on 50 (12:57).
Dorsett gained 11, sweeping left, for a first down on SF 39.
White passed to Springs for 12, for a first down on SF 27.
Dorsett gained 6.
White passed to Crosbie for 21 and a touchdown.

Septien's conversion made score Dallas 27, San Francisco 21 (10:41).
    Ring returned Septien's kickoff 16 yards from the SF 1.
    San Francisco ball, 1/10, on SF 17.
    Montana's pass incomplete.
    Montana passed to Clark for 18 and a first down on SF 35.
    Walls intercepted Montana's pass for Solomon on D 27.
Dallas ball, 1/10, on D 27 (10:07).
Dorsett was stopped for no gain by Harper and Williamson.
Dorsett gained 2, sweeping left.
White passed to Saldi for 9 and a first down on D 38.
White passed to Jones for 4.
Dorsett gained 5, sweeping right.
Springs gained 1, up the middle, for a first down on D 48.
Dorsett gained 2, up the middle.
Dorsett gained 3, on a pitchout right.
White's pass incomplete.
White's 36-yard punt was taken by Solomon on a fair catch.
    San Francisco ball, 1/10, on SF 11 (4:54).
    Montana's pass incomplete.
    Elliott gained 6, up the middle.
    Montana passed to Solomon for 6 and a first down on SF 23.
    Elliott gained 7, sweeping left.
    Montana's pass incomplete.
    Elliott gained 4 but Dallas was penalized 5 yards for offside, giving San
       Francisco a first down on SF 46.
    Montana passed to Cooper for 5.
    Two-minute warning.
    Solomon gained 14 on a reverse around left end, for a first down on D 35.
    Montana passed to Clark for 10 for a first down on D 25.
    Montana passed to Solomon for 12 and a first down on D 13.
    San Francisco took its first timeout (1:15).
    Montana's pass incomplete in end zone.
    Elliott gained 7, sweeping left.
    San Francisco took its second timeout (0:58).
    Montana passed to Clark for 6 and a touchdown.
    Wersching's conversion made score San Francisco 28, Dallas 27 (0:51).
Newsome returned Wersching's kickoff 14 yards from the D 11.
Dallas ball, 1/10, on D 25 (0:46)
White passed to Pearson for 31 and a first down on SF 44.
Dallas took its second timeout (0:38).
White was sacked by Pillers for loss of 7 and fumbled. Stuckey recovering.
San Francisco ball, 1/10, on 50 (0:30).
Montana downed the ball for loss of 3.
Dallas took its third timeout (0:27).
Montana downed the ball for loss of 4 as time ran out.

Walsh turns doorman

In Southfield, Mich., Bill Walsh stood in the lobby of the San Francisco 49ers' hotel, wearing a doorman's coat (42 long), tattered gloves and a hat three sizes too small for his head. The imp in his soul had gained temporary control of his personality, but only on the surface. Beneath the ridiculous outfit, the football coach in him already was thinking of tomorrow and tomorrow and tomorrow. Laughs aside, the Super Bowl still is just a business trip for him.

"Gee, I've got a lot of things to do," he said as he waited for the arrival of his team from the Detroit Metropolitan Airport. "Lots to do, lots to do."

That's the way he planned it. The week of practices and meetings the 49ers concluded in Redwood City Saturday covered only about half of what needs to be done to prepare properly for their Super Bowl foe, the Cincinnati Bengals. Walsh took great care not to leave the best of his team on the West Coast a week before its most important game.

"The workouts by and large were easier than normal last week," he said. "We wanted to come here with a certain amount of work still to be done. We don't want the players to come here and be bored."

Given the wrath of the Arctic storm that locals are calling the "Siberian Express," boredom should be fairly easy to come by here. The temperatures didn't climb above zero until midday today, and the winds at their most genteel have whipped through Michigan at 15 miles per hour. Driving is treacherous, and most people are simply staying indoors. The 49er players might as well be doing the same.

Not on the field, however. Walsh has saved the carbonation in his practices for Michigan.

"I visited with several people and talked to them about this," Walsh said Sunday, several hours before his doorman's gambit. "Some people prepared so much that their players almost became bored when they got to the Super Bowl. So we came here wanting to work on some plays."

Among the coaches with whom he discussed Game Day Minus Six were last year's two finalists, Tom Flores of Oakland and Dick Vermeil of Philadelphia. Walsh wouldn't say exactly what he discussed, but he no doubt talked to Flores for the do's and Vermeil for the don'ts. Vermeil prepared the Eagles so thoroughly last year that he ran them through a full scrimmage four days before the game. Flores, on the other hand, tacitly indicated to his players that anything short of a felony would be forgiven in the interests of staying loose for the game.

Philadelphia practiced well on Wednesday. Oakland won by 17 points on Sunday.

"Tom helped us as much as anybody," Walsh said. "Their (the Raiders) thinking comes closer to ours than anybody else. This is certainly a big trip for us, with tremendously high stakes. We know there are teams that get here and suffer from a stress factor, working too hard and too long. We won't be like that. One of the fortunate things about this team is that it's a business-like team. We've been able to keep our composure on the road, especially when we played in Pittsburgh and Cincinnati.''

In those cities, the 49ers played as well as they have all season in beating two of their most formidable opponents. Part of the secret of winning was in staying loose. Another part was in not becoming so loose as to unravel. There will be a curfew for the players, but nobody in the 49er hierarchy is quite sure who will be checking the naughty against the nice. Maybe nobody will check.

"A curfew is one thing, but a Marine barracks is another," Walsh said. "We haven't had a violation all year as far as I know, but we haven't checked that much either."

There won't be much need for the 49er coaches to check up unless the weather turns balmy in a hurry. The players will find ways to budget their time, most of that time directed at combating the Bengals. Walsh's plan is to keep the players occupied with football just enough to prevent the need for a Wednesday torture session on the Vermeil plan. For Walsh, Super Bowl week is a matter of pacing—a little heavy work here, a little light fun there.

"I'm part of it, I think," Walsh said when asked who was supposed to keep the players from getting too grim. "The coaches and Dwight Clark, Dwight Hicks, they all are very good at that. On the other hand, we have Jack Reynolds, who's all business 12 months a year."

So Walsh stood in the snow waiting for his team, looking a little like a septuagenarian employee of a bowery flop house, because it would be a great gag. The players loved it, at least the ones who recognized him. While he stood there, Walsh thought of Monday, and Tuesday and Wednesday and Thursday as well. He never misses a trick. Like the old vaudeville saw, Walsh always leaves his players wanting a little more. He is determined not to leave the fruit of his labors on the practice field Wednesday for a Sunday game.

Then there was Steve Daley's view:

PONTIAC, Mich.—There are preferred topics here at Super Bowl XVI. The weather, for example.

Writers from California, sensitive types without exception, consider the weather in this part of Michigan downright frigid. This is to be expected. Writers from California consider bean sprouts a vegetable. On that basis alone, they are not to be taken seriously.

Others preferred topics along Interstate 75 include the similarities between quarterbacks Joe Montana of the San Francisco 49ers and Ken Anderson of the Cincinnati Bengals, the differences between coaches Bill Walsh and Forrest Gregg, as well as the mysterious Emerald City, Detroit.

At this Super Bowl, the yellow brick road does not lead to the Motor City. Detroit is a rumor, a $15 cab ride to nowhere. At the press hotel in Dearborn, there is an unofficial $100 fine for leaving the premises.

Then there are the geniuses. Bill Walsh is one, and so is Paul Brown, founder of the Cincinnati Bengals and second in command to George Halas as pro football's patriarch.

Lindy Infante, the Bengals' quarterback coach, is considered a sort of semigenius, and by the end of the week, the sporting press may have anointed a few more. What do you do with Edward J. DeBartolo Jr.?

DeBartolo is president of the San Francisco 49ers, and thanks to his father, principal owner of the franchise.

In 1979, DeBartolo the Younger hired Bill Walsh away from Stanford University and made him 49er head coach and general manager. So what does that make DeBartolo?

DeBartolo did that shortly after firing one-time football maven Joe Thomas. The wizard of Miami and Baltimore had taken several years to wreck the operation with trades that would be embarrassing even in Chicago.

Three years ago, folks in the San Francisco Bay Area were talking about running the poor little rich kid out of town. That, of course, was before Walsh was signed on, before the team went 2–14 to 6–10 to the Super Bowl.

So why isn't anybody draping the mantle of genius around DeBartolo's puny shoulders?

It may have something to do with DeBartolo's image. He doesn't look like a genius.

Looking the part does account for something in this business. Paul Brown looks like somebody carved him off the side of a mountain, but he didn't hire Walsh when he had the chance in 1975.

"Bill was pretty well known in the Bay Area when he was at Stanford," DeBartolo said Wednesday morning. "After he won the Bluebonnet Bowl over Georgia in '78, a lot of people were talking about him."

DeBartolo, having divested himself of Thomas, presented Walsh with an unorthodox opportunity. In essence, he handed the club over to him as coach and general manager.

Walsh surrounded himself with some high-powered deputies, men like former New York Giant's coach John McVay and former Denver Broncos' coach John Ralston. He put DeBartolo in the shade, much as Thomas had done.

The difference was simple. Walsh made the owner like it. And he started to win football games.

"My philosophy, if you want to call it that, is simply a support function," DeBartolo said.

"I don't want to call any plays. I like to be in on what's going on, but Bill has complete autonomy to decide what goes on with the football team."

DeBartolo lives in Youngstown, Ohio, close by the real estate, shopping mall and development empire constructed by his father, Edward J. DeBartolo the Elder. The notion of buying a football team, according to Junior, came from his father.

"It was my dad's idea from the beginning," he said. "It came up over coffee about six o'clock one morning in Youngstown. That night I was on a plane to San Francisco with a lawyer. He met with the team owners, the Morabito ladies, the next day. The whole process took about two weeks, I think."

DeBartolo does not have much to say about his father's impact on the 49ers operation. Surely the old man had something to say during the bad old days, the 2–14 days?

A funny little smile works at the corners of Junior's mouth when that possibility is broached.

"What did my father say? 'Bite the bullet, kid. Get the right people around you.'"

"The first time I sat down and talked to Walsh, I knew he could turn this around," DeBartolo said. "There was something about him, a confidence, a self-assurance that told me I didn't have to look any further."

DeBartolo was right, and not for the last time. In the cloud of superlatives settling over Pontiac this week, it is easy to forget that Walsh, in his first season, duplicated the 2–14 season turned in by Thomas and company in 1978.

"I never had any doubts about Bill, even in the low moments," the NFL's youngest magnate insisted.

"I made mistakes when Joe was running the club," DeBartolo said. "He changed a lot of things within the organization, and I should have been more aware of what was going on. All you can do is try to learn something."

Learn something, and maybe hire Bill Walsh. If he gets a little gray in his hair, someone might even start calling Junior a genius.

Chapter 4

The Best Season

There was cautious optimism when the San Francisco 49ers opened their pre-season training camp at Sierra College in Rocklin last July.

But there were also question marks. Coach Bill Walsh had to solve a problem at quarterback. And he had to decide if it was worth the gamble to start three rookies in the defensive secondary.

What about linebacker Jack Reynolds, obtained from the Los Angeles Rams? Was he over the hill at 34?

Walsh knew he had most of the pieces of a contending team. But he had to put them together and then decide if anything was missing.

There were almost 100 players when camp opened and that number had to be pared to 45 in six weeks.

The veterans were in a main dormitory building at the college and most of the rookies were in an annex. The rookies' names were on their doors, written on a piece of adhesive tape.

Some days, after practice, names would disappear from doors. Free agent Saladin Martin, a defensive back from San Diego State, and rookie Henry Williams, a wide receiver from Long Beach State, shared a room.

One morning, Williams' name was gone. So was Williams. But Martin played the entire season with the 49ers.

There were early hints the 49ers might be better than people expected. Quarterback Joe Montana looked very good in practice. There were rumors Steve DeBerg, the starting quarterback for most of the 1980 season, would be traded for a running back.

Among the names mentioned were Rob Carpenter of the Houston Oilers (who later was traded to the New York Giants) and Ricky Bell of the Tampa Bay Buccaneers.

The 49ers didn't get Carpenter or Bell, but they found someone else.

Out on the practice field, a stubby kid from Carlmont High School and Brigham Young University knew the 49ers were looking for a running back. Each day he did his best, but no one seemed to notice.

Bill Walsh noticed. Bill Ring became a backup running back and a key member of the special teams.

Walsh also remembered players who did the job for him when he was the coach at Stanford. He signed two of them—defensive end Milt McColl and defensive back Rick Gervais—as free agents.

Both made it to the Super Bowl.

George Seifert, the defensive backfield coach, was convinced his rookies could do the job as starters in the National Football League. There were skeptics.

Don't rookie defensive backs make at least one serious mistake a game?

Seifert didn't think Ronnie Lott from USC, Carlton Williamson from Pittsburgh and Eric Wright from Missouri would make many mistakes.

"Ronnie Lott is the best young defensive back I have ever seen," Siefert said before Lott ever had played in a pro game. "He has the ability to run with the receiver, then make the correct defensive play at just the right time."

Quite simply, the 49ers would not be champions if Lott had not made the correct plays.

Seifert realized Williamson was almost as good as Lott.

"He's very good on coverage for a big man. He's tenacious and hits hard when he goes after the ball."

Wright impressed Seifert with how quickly he made the adjustment from college to pro football.

"He makes all the right moves." Seifert said.

The Jack Reynolds situation was quite different. Here was a linebacker who had played in the Pro Bowl twice and was an eight-year starter for the Los Angeles Rams.

Even his teammates were in awe of the man with the nickname of "Hacksaw." He was one tough dude.

Reynolds refused to talk about his past as a Ram.

In a rare interview in Rocklin, Reynolds encapsulated his philosophy of football.

"All I ask is that everyone does his job. When

I'm playing football, I don't have time to worry about what anyone else is doing.

"When I go on the field, it's to play football. I play the best I can and that's all I can do. When the game is over, I ask myself if I did the job."

In answer to those questions, Reynolds did the job this season.

Toward the end of training camp, Walsh had a very good idea of what he still needed to make the 49ers a playoff team.

Those needs were an experienced offensive tackle, a quarterback-sacking defensive lineman and a running back who could get first downs or touchdowns in the tough situations.

Offensive tackle Dan Audick was obtained in a trade with the San Diego Chargers. James Owens, Walsh's first draft choice who never quite made it, went to Tampa Bay for running back Johnny Davis.

When the season started, Walsh still needed one more player. He knew who he wanted, but wasn't quite sure how to get him.

The player was Fred Dean, a very talented but unhappy defensive end for the Chargers.

After losing two of the first four regular-season games, Walsh decided he had to have Dean.

A deal was worked out and Dean became a 49er on Oct. 2. He made his debut for San Francisco in a 45-14 victory over the Dallas Cowboys Oct. 11.

The 49ers have won 14 of 15 games since Dean joined the team.

At the time, however, no one knew what lay ahead. The four pre-season games were entertaining, but not terribly revealing. There was a 27-24 victory in overtime at Seattle, a 31-28 end-of-game loss to San Diego at Candlestick, another victory over Seattle (24-17 at home) and a 21-7 loss at Oakland.

This was poor material for drawing conclusions. Seattle was coming off a 4-12 season and its star quarterback had injury problems. San Diego was an acknowledged powerhouse, and playing the Chargers even might be considered an encouraging sign—if one could forget that in each of the two preceding seasons, the 49ers had beaten San Diego in pre-season games before San Diego went on to win its division with 12-4 and 11-5 records, while the 49ers went on to finish 2-14 and 6-10. Evidently, exhibition game results didn't prove much.

This proved to be especially true with regard to the Raiders. In 1980, in the opening pre-season game, the 49ers had piled up a 33-0 lead in a 33-14 victory—and the Raiders, it turned out, ended that season as Super Bowl champions. Now the Raiders had beaten the 49ers almost as handily.

Did that mean that the 49ers were startlingly worse than they had been the year before?

No. It meant that the Raider-49er loser goes on to win the Super Bowl. So much for exhibition games as indicators.

At least one observer, however, got valid impressions. Al Davis, principal owner, former coach and absolute boss of the Raiders, was asked how good he thought the 49ers were when they routed the Raiders in 1980. "Better than they were, but not very good," he said. "Our team is much better." But when his defending-champion Raiders stifled the 49ers in 1981, his comment was: "They've made tremendous improvement and they're going to have a fine year."

He didn't know how fine, and neither did anyone else.

The first regular-season game, in Detroit, was considered a key game by the 49ers. The prevailing view of the coming season was: Atlanta and Los Angeles, the two powerful teams of the recent past, would fight it out again for first place in the Western Division. New Orleans, under a new coach, would certainly improve on the 1-15 season it had in 1980. The 49ers, depending so heavily on their rookie defensive players and inexperienced quarterback, would be concerned with internal improvement, not pennant race. If they could go 8-8, which would be their first non-losing record in five years, it would represent progress satisfactory to all concerned. Then another good draft could make the team a contender in 1982.

And to reach 8-8, it seemed a victory in Detroit would be needed. The way the schedule broke, the 49ers would be alternating home-away almost entirely. A road victory at the start, against a team that didn't seem out of their class, could set up the morale and the numbers to withstand probable over-matchings later on.

It was this context that made the opening loss so disturbing.

An unpublicized injury had a disproportionate effect and—eventually—much ironic importance. Ray Wersching had pulled a muscle high in his leg and could not place-kick normally. This affected both the strategy and the physical play at vital times—and led to the discovery of the bounding kickoffs that would prove so valuable in the Super Bowl.

Still, Wersching was able to kick a 25-yard field goal that gave the 49ers a 3-0 lead in a desultory first half. They still had it in the final minute when Billy Sims turned a little pass into a 39-yard scoring play. And when Arrington Jones fumbled the kickoff on the San Francisco 25, the Lions kicked a field goal and went off leading 10-0.

The 49er offense got moving in the third quarter, and chewed up the period with two long drives. The first ended in a missed field goal attempt by the injured Wersching. The second tied the game at 10-10 on play into the final quarter.

By now Wersching couldn't even try to kick. Jones, in his place, kicked short and Detroit marched to a touchdown. The 49ers marched right back and made it 17-17 with 7:30 to play. Again, a short kickoff let Detroit start on its 38, so that a punt pinned the Niners down inside their 15, and after the return punt, Detroit started on the 50 with 4:09 left. Ball control and a field goal would have been enough to win, but the Lions worked it down to the one-yard line with 22 seconds left, and Sims scored on third down.

Flying home from Detroit, no one thought there would be a happier flight over the same route four and a half months later.

Wersching had to be placed on the injured reserve list, for a minimum of four games, to heal. The 49ers signed Matt Bahr, recently cut by the

Pittsburgh Steelers, as an avowed temporary measure. The need to win the home opener, against the Chicago Bears, was now greater than ever, to avoid an 0-2 start (with a trip to Atlanta coming up) and the possibility of a downward slide.

The 49ers did beat the Bears, 28-17, and certain patterns emerged that were to be repeated later, with more notice.

One was an effective, long first-quarter march for the game's first touchdown, and a 14-0 lead early in the second. Scoring first was to become a key characteristic of the 49er success right through the Super Bowl.

But, as would happen again, the early lead was not used to put the game out of reach, but as an eventual cushion against counterattack. A wild center snap through Montana's legs, giving the Bears the ball on the San Francisco 4, gave Chicago a gift touchdown, and it was only 14-10 at halftime. On the first possession of the second half, Chicago went ahead, 17-14.

And here came the second pattern that was to make the season what it was: having lost the lead, the 49ers took it back and held it. A recovered fumble on the Chicago 33, a long pass, a short pass and the 49ers led, 21-17, still in the third quarter. A 50-yard march off an interception applied the clincher during the last five minutes of the game.

The third pattern had to do with running backs. Walter Payton, Chicago's superstar, was contained reasonably well, and that was enough against a team committed to using him as its chief weapon.

The visit to Atlanta seemed to confirm all pessimistic skepticism about Walsh's famous rebuilding program, and aggravated widespread impatience among the fans. Atlanta led 17-0 in the first 11 minutes, and 34-17 at the end of the day.

But those who paid closer attention (including, of course, the 49er coaches and players) came away feeling optimistic.

It hadn't really been a one-sided game, and at the time Atlanta was still considered a powerhouse, one of the two or three strongest teams in the league. If the 49ers could play them substantially even, in a physical sense, it meant the 49ers were a lot better than they had been.

What happened in the game was this. At the start, two sustained Atlanta drives produced a touchdown and a field goal, and Ronnie Lott's fumble of the next kickoff on the 21 set up another touchdown. But Montana took the 49ers 80 yards for their own touchdown, and Bahr kicked a 47-yard field goal on the next possession, so it was 17-10. The Falcons marched back for 24-10, but Montana also got a good drive going, from his 8 to the Atlanta 7, where Barr missed just before the half ended.

From the second half kickoff, the 49ers marched effectively again, to the Atlanta 5—where Tom Pridemore picked off Montana's third-down pass in the end zone and took it 101 yards for a touchdown the other way. That made it 31-17 instead of 24-17, and settled the issue for that day, but didn't alter the fact that the 49ers had made a strong showing.

The next game, at home, was not a strong showing. They beat New Orleans, 21-14, but left themselves dissatisfied. George Rogers, the star rookie running back of the Saints, was not contained, and the 49ers were fortunate that New Orleans decided to use its rookie quarterback, Dave Wilson, the first three quarters. It was 7-7 at the half, and it took a 60-yard pass play to Fred Solomon to put San Francisco ahead early in the third quarter. When the Saints switched to Archie Manning with only 13 minutes left, Lott intercepted a deflected pass and ran it in for a touchdown and a 21-7 lead. Manning then conducted an 80-yard scoring drive, and the 49ers wound up hanging on to the ball to kill the final minute.

The 49ers felt they could play better, and would have to.

Washington was the next stop. The Redskins were already 0-4, but somehow ranked at the top of the statistics both offensively and defensively. They were considered a formidable opponent on the road.

Instead, what occurred was the Atlanta game in reverse.

The opening drive went 80 yards for a 49er touchdown.

On Washington's counterattack, Dwight Hicks picked off a fumble forced by Lott and ran 80 yards for another touchdown.

After an exchange of field goals, another 49er march (64 yards) made it 24-3 at the half.

And it went to 30-3, on an interception touchdown by Lott, before Washington scored twice in the final quarter. The final score was 30-17.

Coming home to play mighty Dallas, the 49ers had a 3-2 record. That was exactly the same record they carried into the Dallas game the year before—and Dallas won that one, 59-14. This time, the 49ers would have home field advantage, but few people thought that would made up a 45-point differential. At Washington, everything had broken right, and there was no disposition to look a gift horse in the mouth; but real respectability could come only by proving competitive equality with a team like the Cowboys.

It turned out to be the worst mismatch of the year—for Dallas.

This was the game in which Fred Dean was unleashed. This was the game in which the mushiness of the Candlestick field, especially where the baseball infield had been resodded, became a big issue. This was the game in which the 49er ability to stifle great running backs, hinted at in the Walter Payton game, was established against Tony Dorsett.

And it was the first game in many years in which a 49er team absolutely dominated an opponent.

The sequence was spectacular, and provoked the first real feeling that something special might be in the making.

San Francisco's first two possessions were long touchdown drives. A forced fumble on the Dallas 6 set up a 21-0 margin still in the first quarter. An interception set up a short drive to a field goal (by Wersching, who returned to action in this game). Dallas did manage to work its way to a score before halftime, but early in the third quarter Montana hit Clark on a 78-yard scoring play and Lott took an interception for a 41-yard touchdown. It was 38-7 and a nine-minute 89-yard march made it 45-7

The Sod Squad at work at Candlestick Park

before Dallas got its other score on a 72-yard fumble return.

Final score, 45-14—a turnaround of 76 points in one years.

For the 49er Faithful, no further convincing was necessary: they would go straight to the Super Bowl.

For all the "rational" people, and especially the experts who laughed at such naive enthusiasm, the question was still how well might the 49ers do in their own division. Any team can have a hot game. Would the 49ers, as so many teams did, react to it by losing to a weaker team the following week?

The weaker team was Green Bay, the game was in Milwaukee, and the weather was wet and miserable. The newly appreciated 49er defense did its job, and after a 3-3 first half, it never let the Packers reach midfield while the offense punched across a third-period touchdown and a fourth-quarter field goal.

This 13-3 victory, in its way, was as important as the Dallas rout, because it displayed the even-keel consistency that would emerge as this team's greatest asset.

And the 5-2 record put the 49ers in first place in their division, a division in which the Rams and Falcons were running into unforeseen troubles of their own.

The Rams represented a special frustration for all San Francisco fans. The cultural (and regional) hostility between the two cities was old stuff to stand-up comics, sociologists and newspaper columnists, but to sports fans there were extra elements. The baseball Dodgers, the basketball Lakers and the football Rams kept winning their share of championships, often at the expense of the Giants, the Warriors and the 49ers, who didn't. Even in college sports, USC in football and UCLA in basketball usually beat up on Stanford and Cal-Berkeley. When it came to intra-California competition, the north was always finishing second.

For the 49ers in particular, the Rams were THE rival. In the middle 1970s, the 49ers had won a couple of games in Los Angeles, but they had not beaten the Rams in San Francisco, before the eyes of their home fans, since 1966. They had never, in fact, beaten the Rams at Candlestick Park, which became their home in 1971. That 1966 game had been at long abandoned (and fondly remembered) Kezar Stadium.

Now they would take a four-game winning streak—the longest they had ever produced under Walsh—against the Rams at Candlestick. To their followers, even more than to the 49ers themselves, this was the test of faith: the Dallas game had been a delight, but obviously just one of those things. To beat the Rams—that would MEAN something.

The field was at its soggiest, and that was to prove important. Midway through the first period, the Rams reached the San Francisco 22, but a couple of five-yard penalties forced Frank Corral to try a 49-yard field goal, and he didn't make it.

Montana promptly engineered a 68-yard drive, and the 49ers had what was becoming their customary 7-0 lead.

On the answering series, the Rams decided to try for a first down on fourth-and-one on the San Francisco 43, and Dwight Hicks nailed Cullen Bryant for a four-yard loss. Four plays later, Montana and Clark connected on a 41-yard touchdown and the lead was 14-0.

The next Ram drive reached the San Francisco 31, and ended with an interception by Lott on the 7. The Rams had now gained 105 yards in 17 minutes, and didn't have a point to show for it.

Nor could the 49ers keep them from moving the ball. From the ensuing punt, the Rams got to the 8, where the 49er defense forced them to settle for a field goal. The next time they got the ball, they were able to grind out a five-minute, 16-play, 96-yard drive for 14-10, with only a minute to go in the half. But the 49ers used that minute for a 50-yard gain on a pass to Earl Cooper and a 42-yard field goal by Wersching, so the second half began 17-10.

Five minutes into the third period, the Rams were down on the San Francisco 8 again. Corral tried a 26-yard field goal—and Dwaine Board blocked it.

Montana engineered a patient drive that covered 79 yards to the Los Angeles 1, on fourth down. Coach Walsh elected to take the three points, and Wersching made it 20-10.

Four minutes later it was 20-17, after a 66-yard Ram advance in only five plays, and there was still the whole fourth quarter to play.

The real drama began here. The 49ers never did make another first down. The 49er defense had already given up 348 yards in three quarters. It was strictly a battle for survival.

The first Ram possession ended in a sack and a punt.

So did the next, with Lawrence Pillers chasing Pat Haden for a 16-yard loss on the sack.

The next time, the Rams reached a fourth-and-one on the San Francisco 14 with six minutes left. They elected to try to tie the game. Corral had a 32-yard attempt, off bad footing, and he missed—but not by much. The ball hit the right goal post, then the crossbar, and fell back into the end zone instead of over.

Moments later the Rams were back on the San

Francisco 34—and again the third-down play was a sack, this one by Fred Dean. Corral had to punt, and the 49ers had to punt back. With 2:03 to play, the Rams had time to mount a winning drive.

Undeterred by two sacks, Haden completed a 33-yard pass to the San Francisco 31, just inside the last minute. A field goal would avert immediate defeat and force overtime, and momentum was certainly with the Rams if they could reach an extra period. On fourth-and-seven from the 28, with the clock showing 0:17, Corral kicked a 45-yard placement—wide left.

The 20-17 lead had held.

Was the world convinced? Not yet. The next assignment was in Pittsburgh, where the Steelers had not lost to a National Conference team in 10 years.

Walsh and his staff looked upon this as a new kind of test. The two great victories so far, Dallas and Los Angeles, had been at home. This game would be in a hostile environment, against a notably "physical" team of great experience. The emotional situation, after the Rams, was ripe for a letdown in traditional football terms, but the 49ers knew they weren't in an up-and-down rollercoaster syndrome, even if outsiders didn't. No, this was going to be a physical problem, not a psychological one.

And the 49ers passed the test brilliantly.

It was a homecoming for Joe Montana, who grew up in nearby Monangahela—and Joe was hurt. His ribs were banged up, breathing was painful, and a flak jacket was procured for him to wear.

It cut down on the freedom of his throwing motion, and although the secret was well kept until after the game, there was some question about how much he would be able to play.

The hitting was fierce from the start—and the 49ers, especially those young defensive backs, were doing the hardest hitting. The only scoring threat of the first 28 minutes ended when Franco Harris fumbled on the San Francisco 23 midway through the first quarter.

With two minutes to go in the half, an interception let the 49ers start on their own 46. They made it to the end zone, on a five-yard pass to Charle Young, with 32 seconds left. And when Carlton Williamson pounced on a fumble on the Pittsburgh 37 on the first play after the kickoff, Wersching got a shot at a 45-yarder and made it, for a 10-0 lead.

Montana, concentrating on short passes, had been nearly perfect the first half. As he took the 49ers toward midfield on the first possession of the second half, he had 16 completions in 23 tries. But his next pass was intercepted and returned 50 yards for a touchdown by Mel Blount. And on the next series, he was intercepted again, by Jack Lambert, who ran it back 31 yards to the 22, and one pass from Terry Bradshaw had Pittsburgh ahead, 14-10, just like that.

This, then, was test time.

Montana got back on track, moved the team 69 yards to the Pittsburgh 20, but came up empty as Wersching's field goal attempt was blocked.

The 49er defense promptly forced a fumble and

got the ball back. The 49er offense couldn't gain, so after the punt, the defense got it back again, on an interception by Williamson, who ran 28 yards to the Pittsburgh 43.

And this time, Montana took them in, with Walt Easley covering the last 13 yards on four running plays, with 5:35 left.

Leading 17-14, the 49ers could be caught by a field goal or beaten by a touchdown, and the Steelers moved powerfully from their 17 to the San Francisco 34, where it was third and one. There, a fierce pass rush turned a completion into a two-yard loss, and another forced an incompletion on fourth down.

The winning streak was up to six, and credibility was taking root.

Yet the schedule was only one game past its midpoint, and the game coming up seemed as difficult as any: the return match with Atlanta, this time at Candlestick. After all, the last two times the teams met—late in 1980 and early in 1981—the Falcons had won by scores of 35-10 and 34-17. Atlanta, it was true, had lost four of six games since beating the 49ers, and had a 5-4 record against San Francisco's 7-2. But its last game was a 41-10 rout of New Orleans and it seemed ready to tighten the race.

But the pattern held.

In the first 26 minutes, nobody scored. One promising 49er drive, to the Atlanta 26, ended in an interception. An Atlanta advance to the San Francisco 28 ended in a missed field goal.

Then—whoosh—the 49ers had their standard

7-0 lead in two plays. A pass to Clark gained 44 yards, with 14 more tacked on because Montana was roughed. A 14-yard pass to Solomon scored.

With only seconds left in the first half, Hicks took an interception to the San Francisco 45, Montana hit Solomon on the Atlanta 31, and Wersching kicked a 45-yard field goal as time expired.

Atlanta closed to within 10-7 with an eight-minute drive in the third period, but the 49ers opened the fourth quarter with a 77-yard drive of their own for 17-7. That seemed safe enough when the clock got down to 2:23 with Atlanta in possession on its own 24.

It wasn't going to be that easy, however. A flurry of passes by Steve Bartkowski covered 76 yards in only 40 seconds, and it was 17-14 with an onside kick sure to be attempted.

The 49ers grabbed it—but were offside.

Atlanta recovered the next one—but it was offside.

Mick Luckhurst tried it a third time—and Atlanta got it and kept it on the San Francisco 42.

And a 25-yard pass put it on the 17 with 1:23 to go.

The Falcons now had three shots at a winning touchdown before having to try for a tying field goal.

But Hicks intercepted Bartkowski's next pass, and the defense had done it again.

The 49ers now had a seven-game winning streak, not only a club record but an amazing sequence of hard-fought close calls. There had just been three 3-point victories in a row against formidable opponents, and the 49ers had notched four victories while scoring only seven touchdowns.

And the next week, at Candlestick, they didn't score any. The field was softer than ever and the Cleveland Browns, having a poor season, didn't seem imposing. Their place-kicker was Bahr, traded to them by the 49ers when Wersching returned, and their quarterback, Brian Sipe, was having a tough time.

Early in the game, Montana was charged with a safety for throwing the ball away under a pass rush in his own end zone, but four field goals by Wersching did let the 49ers take a 12-5 lead into the middle of the fourth quarter.

This time, however, the magic ran out. A 40-yard punt return and some crisp passes by Sipe produced the tying touchdown with 6:46 left. The Niners stalled and punted, and Sipe took his team, methodically, as far as the San Francisco 4 before Bahr kicked the winning field goal at 0:43.

The 15-12 defeat was to be the third and last of the entire season.

The same day, both Atlanta and Los Angeles lost, so the 49ers remained in command in their division. But the Rams were next in line, and if the 49er hot streak was really running out, the race could get tight again in a hurry.

Instead, November 22 at Anaheim became one of the most memorable days of all.

Dan Pastorini was the Ram quarterback now, and the 49ers showed no more ability to keep the Rams from piling up yardage than they had in their first meeting. A 47-yard field goal by Wersching gave the 49ers the first score, but Corral matched it with a 44-yarder in the first minute of the second period. Pastorini conducted an 80-yard drive the next time the Rams had the ball, for 10-3, and Montana matched it in fewer plays with passes of 44 and 28 yards to Solomon, setting up a one-yard touchdown for Johnny Davis. Then Pastorini used up the rest of the half with another 80-yard march, and the 49ers went off trailing 17-10.

It was the first time in 10 weeks that they had trailed at halftime, since the game in Atlanta.

Not for long, though. Amos Lawrence took the second-half kickoff 92 yards for a touchdown.

The next possession produced a field goal, and San Francisco led, 20-17. By mid-period it was 27-17 as Lott intercepted Pastorini for a touchdown. The Rams switched to Haden at quarterback.

That worked, for he promptly passed his way to a touchdown that made it 27-24 going into the fourth quarter.

Wersching kicked his third field goal of the game, for 30-24, but Haden took command. Using up eight minutes, he moved the Rams 90 yards to a touchdown that enabled Corral's extra point to "win" the game, 31-30, with only 1:51 left.

What it really did, however, was create what has since become recognized as Joe Montana Time.

Cramming 13 plays into 109 seconds, Montana drove his team from 20 to 20 (actually, to the Ram 19). With two seconds left, he put the ball down for Wersching's 37-yard kick, which was on target as usual, and the 49ers won, 33-31.

They had beaten the Rams twice in one year for

the first time since 1965. The Los Angeles demon had been exorcised. And a spot in the playoffs was assured.

To clinch first place in the division, and avoid the possibility of a wild-card game in the preliminary round, they had to beat the New York Giants at Candlestick.

They didn't do it easily, but they did it, 17-10. Again, they got a 14-0 lead in 18 minutes, and led 14-3 at the half. When the Giants made it 14-10 on the first play of the fourth quarter, after a long march, Walsh called on Paul Hofer to make the key runs and catches in a 7½ minute sequence that led to a point-blank field goal and a safer margin.

With first place clinched, a furor arose about the upcoming visit to Cincinnati, where the Bengals had not yet clinched their division title. A remark by Walsh, misreported, fed speculation that 49er regulars would be "rested." In fact, 49er players knew how deeply Walsh felt about facing the team that had rejected him as head coach years before. They went to Cincinnati in a high sense of readiness, and produced an overpowering performance.

All the now familiar patterns were there: first score (long drive after an interception on the first possession), strong defense against the run, forced turnovers, a bewildering attack pattern. The Bengals got a field goal with 2:32 to go in the half, so Montana used the remaining time to make it 14-3, passing to Clark for the last 15 yards of an 80-yard move.

The rest of the game was spent frustrating the Cincinnati offense, and it ended 21-3 as fumble recovery set up a fourth-quarter move of 40 yards for the final 49er touchdown (on a one-yard run by Montana).

Only two games remained, pressure-free but desirable to win to nail down possible home-field rights for playoff games. Houston was stifled, 28-6, although the first half was 0-0 and reserves played freely in building a 28-0 lead. The shutout held until the final minute.

By the time the last scheduled game started at New Orleans, the 49ers had home field clinched, since Dallas had lost its game on Saturday, so this was strictly for exercise. But winning is supposed to become a habit, and for the 49ers it had. A typical opening drive under Montana made it 7-0. A fumbled punt and a fumbled kickoff let New Orleans go ahead, 14-7, on advances of only 18 and 7 yards, but Montana conducted another 69 yard march for 14-14 before turning the reins over to Guy Benjamin for the rest of the day. The Saints went ahead again on a third-quarter field goal, but Benjamin guided a fourth-quarter drive to 21-17; and when the Saints threatened to answer it, Williamson's interception quashed that idea once and for all.

The numbers were indelible: 13 games won, 3 lost, the best record in the league in 1981, the best in the National Conference since the schedule had been lengthened to 16 games in 1978, the best season by far in 49er history—and the real excitement was just beginning.

Chapter 5

The New 49ers

By finishing first in their division, the 49ers were able to enjoy the best of both worlds. In the National Football League, being "home for Christmas" usually means a team failed to make the playoffs, since that's the weekend playoffs begin. Teams consider the lost holiday well worth the success represented by the need (and right) to keep playing. For the 49ers, though, there was a first-round bye and a home game on January 3, which meant that they could have Christmas at home, with a couple of days off from practice, *and* success.

The first assignment then turned out to be a rematch with the Giants, rather than a first meeting with Philadelphia under Dick Vermeil, one of Walsh's closest friends. The Giants upset the Eagles in Philadelphia in the first playoff game a Giant team had qualified for in 18 years, and the January 3 game became a clash of two upwardly-mobile programs.

Its significance for the 49ers, beyond the competition itself, was that it finally focused the full

Reynolds, Lott, and Pillers study defensive strategy

attention of New York-based media on San Francisco.

The final score, 38-24, simultaneously did and did not reflect the character of the game. The Giants were within four yards of a tie in the third quarter, but in retrospect, it was a fairly one-sided game in which the 49ers had control all the way.

An opening drive of 85 yards, kept alive by a penalty that nullified a 49er punt, gave San Francisco its 7-0 lead. But a 72-yard touchdown pass by Scott Brunner to Earnest Gray—the kind of play the Giants weren't supposed to be able to make and that the 49er secondary wasn't supposed to give up—made it 7-7.

On the first play of the second quarter, Wersching's 22-yard field goal regained the lead. A deflected interception stopped the Giants, and a 58-yard scoring pass to Solomon made it 17-7. A Giant fumble, a 25-yard scoring run by Ricky Patton, and it was 24-7, less than five minutes into the second period. The rout was on.

Well, not quite. The Giants did march to a field goal before halftime, and struck with another not-supposed-to-happen bomb, a 59-yard touchdown from Brunner to Johnny Perkins, early in the third quarter. Now within 24-17, they sacked Montana, forced a punt, and moved 67 yards to third-and-three on the San Francisco 4.

Here Wright knocked the tying touchdown out of Gray's hands on the goal line, in a fine bit of pass defense—and Joe Danelo was wide left with his 21-yard field goal try.

That restored momentum to the 49ers. The fourth quarter began with a 42-yard punt returned by Solomon which set up a routine 36-yard scoring sequence for 31-17 (with Bill Ring carrying the last three yards for the touchdown. Later, Lott's 20-yard interception touchdown—his fourth of the year—made it 38-17, and a final touchdown drive by the Giants meant nothing.

What counted most, perhaps, was atmosphere. In this victory, the 49ers looked so confident and dominant that they really began to be perceived as "new" 49ers, of whom victory could be expected, not merely wished for.

Joy reigned in San Francisco, but not unconfined. For one thing, the 49ers had won a first-round playoff game before. For another, a terrible rainstorm hit that night and caused devastating floods and mudslides that put football results into perspective.

For weeks, the wet weather had spoiled not only the Candlestick field but the 49er practice field at Redwood City. On many days, Walsh had been forced to take his team to one of the nearby Stanford practice fields to work. Now, facing preparations for a conference championship game against Dallas, he decided no half-measures would do. He arranged to move everyone down to Anaheim to the Ram training base for four days of practice while the Bay Area tried to cope with its storms. Actually, it was raining in Anaheim too, 400 miles to the south; but the ground there was not supersaturated with water, and the field could be practiced upon effectively even in the rain.

So the airlift was carried out, with media people from all over the country following the team like lemmings off a cliff, and an incidental benefit turned out to be some experience for the 49er players with hotel-based preparation under a publicity spotlight, a mini-version of what Super Bowl week would be like. Walsh didn't have that as a primary reason for the move, but he never denied that the side effect occurred to him and was welcome.

By Friday, both teams were in San Francisco and the Bay Area was whipping itself into a frenzy. The highest hopes clashed with memories of the obstacle Dallas had been in 1970, 1971 and 1972—especially that awful moment in 1972.

On Sunday, the weather was fine, the field wasn't too bad, the result turned out to be perfect, and the pilgrimage to Pontiac that seemed so improbable in August was on.

And, after the Dallas and Super Bowl victories, where did the new 49ers stand?

They had become only the fourth team in football history to win 16 games in a single season—more victories than they had achieved in the preceding four years added together.

They were the first team to go directly from a losing season to a Super Bowl victory.

They were talent-rich in young players, their veterans weren't too old, and they certainly seemed to have crossed permanently the line between perennial also-ran and perennial contender.

Here is a summary of what three years of the Walsh regime had accomplished.

Building a team

A team must be built "primarily" through the draft, conventional football wisdom says, and when Bill Walsh took over the 49ers in 1979 he stressed that this would be his approach.

But "primarily" does not mean "exclusively." The draft must supply the basic talent level of the squad as a whole, but key positions can be filled by trade, and valuable additions can be found among free agents—players drafted by some other team then cut, or players who were never drafted at all.

Year	Drafted (25)	Free agents (15)	Trades (7)
1973	Willie Harper(2)		
1974	Keith Fahnhorst (2A)		
1976	Randy Cross (2A) John Ayers (8) *Paul Hofer (11)		
1977		Ray Wersching	
1978	Dan Bunz (1B) Walt Downing (2) Archie Reese (5A) Fred Quillan (7)		[1]Freddie Solomon
1979	Joe Montana (3) Dwight Clark (10A) *Phil Francis (7)	Dwaine Board *Lenvil Elliott Dwight Hicks Eason Ransom	
1980	Earl Cooper (1A) Jim Stuckey (1B) Keena Turner (2) Jim Miller (3A) Craig Puki (3B) *Ricky Churchman (4A) Bobby Leopold (8)	Ricky Patton Lawrence Pillers *Ken Bungarda *George Visger	[2]Charle Young
1981	Ronnie Lott (1) John Harty (2A) Eric Wright (2B) Carlton Williamson (3) Lynn Thomas (5A) *Pete Kugler (6)	John Choma Walt Easley Saladin Martin Milt McColl Rick Gervais Jack Reynolds Bill Ring Mike Shumann Mike Wilson Allan Kennedy *Gus Parham	[3]Guy Benjamin [4]Dan Audick [5]Johnny Davis [6]Amos Lawrence [7]Fred Dean

*On injured reserve

Trades

[1]Before '78 from Miami with Vern Roberson and two draft choices for Delvin Williams.

[2]Before '80 from a fifth-round choice in '83 from Los Angeles.

[3]Before '81 from New Orleans for future undisclosed draft choice.

[4]Before '81 from a third-round draft choice in '82 from San Diego.

[5]Before '81 from Tampa Bay for James Owens.

[6]Before second game of '81 for a fourth-round draft choice in '84 from San Diego.

[7]Before fifth game of '81 from San Diego for a second pick and option to exchange No. 1 picks in '82.

The present 49ers are an excellent example of how these sources can be blended into an efficient whole.

The key to successful drafting is good judgment in player evaluation. There is widespread agreement about the potential talents of players like Ronnie Lott, who live up to their reputations, but there are only a few chances to get such a player. (After all, that's the whole idea of the draft, to spread talent evenly.) Much more important is to avoid "wasting" a high choice on someone who doesn't make it, and to concentrate on recognizing (or finding) special talents others didn't rate as highly.

The 49ers found Joe Montana in the third round, Dwight Clark in the 10th. They thought more of Carlton Williamson than other organizations did.

However, they weren't fully prepared for the 1979 draft because the Walsh organization moved in only in February, and previous trades had left only two picks in the first four rounds. In 1980, after making Earl Cooper first choice (having traded Wilbur Jackson for two No. 2 slots), they concentrated on defense and got Jim Stuckey, Keena Turner, punter Jim Miller, Craig Puki and Bobby Leopold. In 1981, they concentrated on defensive backs, with results that have become famous.

But they also needed experienced excellence. Jack Reynolds anchored the linebacking. Fred Dean provided pass rush. Dan Audick solved an emergency at offensive tackle, Guy Benjamin became a backup quarterback. Reynolds was, fortunately, a free agent, but future draft choices had to be given for the others. Here, again, correct value judgments are the key.

Finally, Dwight Hicks, Dwaine Board, Lawrence Pillers, Ricky Patton and Eason Ramson are examples of what gold can be mined on the free-agent lists, if you know what you're doing.

Development

The three-year development of the San Francisco 49ers under general manager and coach Bill Walsh, from the worst record in the National Football League (2-14) to the best (13-3), is reflected most vividly in a few key team statistics.

Walsh began with a reputation as an offensive genius and an unproved record for creating strong defense. He took over a squad that was, despite the presence of perhaps a dozen excellent players, talent-poor by NFL standards. He had to do something, as general manager, to make the team instantly palatable to its disgruntled clientele, as well as build toward a sound future.

Since almost all the good talent on hand consisted of offensive players, and since this was his strength anyhow, the palatability aspect was taken care of by producing an attractive, pass-oriented offense that was fun in itself and enabled the 49ers to stay reasonably close until the late stages of games against stronger teams.

But to be a winning team, a strong defense had to be constructed, and that meant getting better personnel, through the draft and in trades.

The chart of the three Walsh-coached seasons shows how thoroughly these steps have been accomplished.

The offense, statistically rich at the start, shows a modest but steady rise, increasing in efficiency more than in numbers.

The defense, no better in 1980 while the wholesale reshuffling of personnel was in progress, took a quantum leap in 1981.

And all those close games lost in 1980 turned into games won in 1981.

The number of touchdowns scored has stayed the same: 35, 37, 37; the number allowed dropped this year to 26 after being at 49 for two years—a cut of nearly 50 percent.

The table shows that 49er passing, which has a built-in high completion average because of Walsh's system, has gone up along a shallow slope. And the proportion of 49er yardage gained by passing has stayed the same. But the number of pass attempts needed to get that proportion of yardage has gone down, to the point where more than half the 49er plays were running plays.

That's a remarkable change, since the 49ers have not had outstanding or injury-free running backs. The great advantage of running plays is that they take up playing time, which helps keep a team's own defense fresh and reduces the time in which the enemy offense can operate. Winning teams have a larger proportion of runs to passes, not because that's the best way for them to score, but because once they are ahead (and winning teams are ahead more of the time than losing teams), it is in their best interest to run the ball.

The reverse side of the coin is shown by the defense. When the 49ers couldn't stop anybody, the first two years, opponents ran the ball 56 percent and 54 percent of the time, getting the clock and fatigue advantages that go with that pattern. In 1981, with their good defense, the 49ers forced the opposition to pass more than half the time.

And that played into the hands of the strong pass rush and spectacular secondary the 49ers developed. Opposing teams completed 66 percent of their passes in 1980, but were cut to 53 percent in 1981. The number of sacks is not dramatically greater, but the number of interceptions is—27 instead of 17—and that reflects the pressure being put on passers to throw sooner, and the good coverage that makes it hard to find an open receiver.

Yet Walsh's own offense always has been low in interceptions (in proportion to attempts) and in sacks suffered, because the safety-valve design of his ball-control pass offense is so well-conceived and so well-drilled.

These factors show up, most clearly of all, in the outcomes of close games. These can be defined as games in which the final margin is seven points or less, because in such a game it is at least theoretically possible to get a tie on the final play.

In 1979, the 49ers lost five of six such games.

In 1980, they lost six of 10.
In 1981, they won nine of eleven.

Developing the 49ers

OFFENSE	1979	1980	1981
Points	308	320	357
Yards	5,573	5,320	5,484
Percentage of yards gained passing	65%	67%	65%
Percentage of passing plays	55%	57%	47%
Pass-completion average	.600	.608	.634
Interceptions	21	26	13
Sacks	17	30	29
Touchdowns scored	35	37	37

DEFENSE	1979	1980	1981
Points	416	415	250
Yards	5,393	5,969	4,763
Percentage of yards gained passing	59%	66%	60%
Percentage of passing plays	44%	46%	51%
Pass-completion average	.594	.661	.531
Interceptions	15	17	27
Sacks	29	31	36
Touchdowns scored	49	49	26

GENERAL CATEGORIES	1979	1980	1981
Games won	2	6	13
Won by 7 points or less	1	4	7
Won by 8 points or more	1	2	6
Games lost	14	10	3
Lost by 7 points or less	5	6	2
Lost by 8 points or more	9	4	1
Net yards per game vs. opponents' net	+9	−40	+45
Time of possession per game	29:22	27:28	31:43

The one-year turnaround of the 49ers, from losing record to league championship, was the greatest such improvement in National Football League history.

All previous Super Bowl winners had come off winning records the preceding year. Some actually had better records the year before they won the ultimate prize. None had to improve by more than three games (as measured by number of defeats) to gain the championship.

The 49ers, in going from 6-10 to 13-3, reduced their losses by seven games—more than twice as big a change as any other champion made.

And in the 45 years of National Football League play before the Super Bowl began (in the 1966 season), only two teams won the league title after having a losing season the year before, and both were special cases during the unsettled period of World War II. Nor did either of those decrease their number of defeats by as big a margin as the 49ers did.

In 1945, the Cleveland Rams went 9-1 and won the playoff game after a 4-6 season in 1944. In 1946, the Chicago Bears, who had been 3-7 in 1945, went 8-2-1 on their way to regaining a championship they had won before the war. In both instances, the changes were due to wholesale turnover of rosters as top players returned from military service.

The 49er turnover, in an era of enormous stability and prosperity for the league as a whole, is that much more remarkable.

How Super Bowl winners did in preceding year

Season	Super Bowl winner	Regular-season record	Previous-season record	Net change in losses
1981	San Francisco	13-3	6-10	−7
1980	Oakland	11-5	9-7	−2
1979	Pittsburgh	12-4	14-2	+2
1978	Pittsburgh	14-2	9-5	−3
1977	Dallas	12-2	11-3	−1
1976	Oakland	13-1	11-3	−2
1975	Pittsburgh	12-2	10-3-1	−1
1974	Pittsburgh	10-3-1	10-4	−1
1973	Miami	12-2	14-0	+2
1972	Miami	14-0	10-3-1	−3
1971	Dallas	11-3	10-4	−1
1970	Baltimore	11-2-1	8-5-1	−3
1969	Kansas City	11-3	12-2	+1
1968	New York Jets	11-3	8-5-1	−2
1967	Green Bay	9-4-1	12-2	+2
1966	Green Bay	12-2	10-3-1	−1

Chapter 6

Bill Walsh

San Francisco 49er head coach Bill Walsh is a living example of the value of apprenticeship, although he feels with considerable justification and a certain amount of passion, that it was carried to excessive length in his case.

The many-sided skills that go into being a successful coach cannot be acquired in any formal course of study. The intellectual side (at which Walsh always has excelled) is only one facet. Motivating people, evaluating talent, organizing activities, dealing with the public, maintaining credibility—such necessities are mastered through experience.

Walsh began the process while still a player at San Jose State, in the early 1950s. His coach there, Bob Bronzan, was struck by the receptivity of Walsh's mind, and used him as an assistant while Walsh was working on a master's degree. Even at that stage, Walsh's coaching potential seemed clear to those who knew him.

Then, in succession, he became a high school head coach, a college assistant working as defensive coordinator, a college assistant working on administrative matters and coaching a freshman team, a college assistant in charge of defensive backs, a pro assistant coaching the backfield, and an offensive coordinator of a newly-formed professional team.

The last-mentioned post, with the Cincinnati Bengals when they became an expansion team in the American Football League in 1968, lasted eight years, and that's the point at which Walsh began to feel over-apprenticed.

The Bengals were the creation of Paul Brown, whose place in football history is that of an unsurpassed innovator and consistent winner. More features of today's professional game can be traced to Brown's methods, with Cleveland in the All-America Conference and later in the National Football League, than to any other single coach. Under Brown, Walsh both learned and produced. By the third year, the Bengals had a winning record; by the sixth, they were in the NFL playoffs. And an outstanding pass offense, directed by Walsh, was the main element.

Walsh himself, as well as many friends and observers, expected to be promoted to head coach when Brown decided to be just the general manager after the 1975 season. Instead, Brown chose Bill Johnson, his offensive line coach. This left Walsh in a dead-end position with the Bengals, and he moved on.

His reputation as a wizard of offense in general, and coaching quarterbacks and receivers in particular, meant he had various opportunities as an assistant. The one he chose was in San Diego.

Bill Walsh's quarterbacks

QB	Team	Years	Comp Avg	Att	Yds/Att	TD	Int
Greg Cook	*Bengals	1969	.538	197	9.41	15	11
Virgil Carter	Bears	1968-69	.471	193	5.76	6	10
	*Bengals	1970-71	.562	500	6.54	19	16
Ken Anderson	*Bengals	1971	.550	131	5.93	5	4
	*Bengals	1972-75	.593	1335	7.63	64	40
Dan Fouts	Chargers	1973-75	.492	308	6.80	16	16
	*Chargers	1976	.579	208	7.06	14	15
Guy Benjamin	Stanford	1974-76	.586	478	7.17	26	28
	*Stanford	1977	.630	330	7.64	19	15
Steve Dils	*Stanford	1977-78	.633	433	7.55	23	15
Steve DeBerg	49ers	1978	.454	302	5.19	8	22
	*49ers	1979-80	.593	899	6.28	29	38
Joe Montana	*49ers	1979-81	.639	784	6.98	35	21

*With Walsh.

NOTES—Cook was Rookie of the Year in 1969. Anderson was a rookie reserve in 1971, then led the league in passing twice from 1972-75. Benjamin led the nation in passing in 1977 and Dils in 1978.

By now, however, Walsh was 45 years old, short of his career goal of being fully in charge of a professional team, and frustrated by the knowledge that many less capable people had been given that opportunity in various places. At that point, Stanford was looking for a new coach, having dismissed Jack Christiansen. Walsh seized the opportunity to come back to Palo Alto (where he had spent three years under John Ralston in an early stage of apprenticeship) and be, for the first time, in total command of a major program.

Walsh's record

Year	Team	Position	Record
1957–59	Washington High	Head coach	15-10-2
1960	California	Def. (Marv Levy)	2-7-1
1961	California	Def. (Marv Levy)	1-8-1
1962	California	Def. (Marv Levy)	1-9
1963	Stanford	Asst. (John Ralston)	3-5
1964	Stanford	Def. (John Ralston)	5-5
1965	Stanford	Def. (John Ralston)	6-3-1
1966	Oakland Raiders	Off. (John Rauch)	8-5-1
1968	Cincinnati Bengals	Off. (Paul Brown)	3-11
1969	Cincinnati Bengals	Off. (Paul Brown)	4-9-1
1970	Cincinnati Bengals	Off. (Paul Brown)	8-6
1971	Cincinnati Bengals	Off. (Paul Brown)	4-10
1972	Cincinnati Bengals	Off. (Paul Brown)	8-6
1973	Cincinnati Bengals	Off. (Paul Brown)	10-4
1974	Cincinnati Bengals	Off. (Paul Brown)	7-7
1975	Cincinnati Bengals	Off. (Paul Brown)	11-3
1976	San Diego Chargers	Off. (Tom Prothro)	6-8
1977	Stanford	Head coach	9-3
1978	Stanford	Head coach	8-4
1979	San Francisco 49ers	Head coach	2-14
1980	San Francisco 49ers	Head coach	6-10
1981	San Francisco 49ers	Head coach	13-3

He was, of course, a rousing success. He installed a pro offense that perfectly suited the Stanford constituency as well as the Stanford playing personnel, and two winning seasons wound up with bowl game victories.

Now he had the pro football world's attention to a greater degree than before. The New York Giants were interested in him, and so were the Los Angeles Rams. But the best opportunity came up closest to home. The 49ers were in desperate straits. In the two years since the DeBartolo family had purchased them and installed Joe Thomas as general manager, they had failed on the field (5-9 and 2-14) but, even more alarming, had alienated a large portion of their followers. When Eddie DeBartolo Jr. dropped Thomas, he needed not only a sound, long-range building program, but instant public relations and a favorable atmosphere for the additional patience his customers would be asked to exercise.

Walsh was uniquely fitted for both tasks, with his Stanford image and success so bright on the local scene. And he was able to get even more than simply the head coaching position: He was given the ultimate authority of general manager as well.

An interview

Bill Walsh went to Pontiac by way of Washington, where he accepted a Coach of the Year Award and met President Reagan. Before he left, he discussed his philosophy.

Q. Coaching a team in the Super Bowl is the apex of achievement in your profession, and as that experience actually approaches, what thoughts about its significance are uppermost in your mind?

A. I really try very hard not to allow any distraction from the normal routine of preparing for a game. I don't mean to use the cliche that "it's just another ball game," but it's terribly important to concentrate on doing the things that have to be done if you're going to be successful, and the things that have to be done are the same ones we've been doing every week during the season. So when I talk to players or others, or even do my own work, I try to push aside any feeling that this is something special.

Q. But don't such thoughts creep in anyhow?

A. Oh, sure they do. When you're alone, or when it's brought up by someone. It's the goal you work toward for years and years, and when it's over, if we've won, I'll be able to sit back and savor it and look at where I am and what happens next. But until then, there's so much to do and such systematic ways of doing it that I don't think of it in those terms.

Q. Do you think you're unusual in looking at it that way?

A. No, I think all coaches concentrate on whatever routines they use going into a game and push other considerations aside.

Q. What are your routines, exactly? What is this "football philosophy" people talk about, and how is it different from any other?

A. It all starts with devising a consistent system. The numbering system for your plays, and the terminology, has to be broad enough to encompass all the things you'll want to do and all the variations that will arise. It has to be practical for the players and coaches who must learn to use it, but able to include all kinds of expansions and adjustments without having to go outside the system in ways that may be confusing.

Q. Don't all football systems seek that?

A. Yes, but there's one mistake that's often made. It can't be too simple, to make it easier to learn or handle. It has to be complex enough to be effective. That's what you seek, what will be effective. When you have that, you try to simplify it as much as possible, but you don't sacrifice effectiveness for the sake of simplicity. You make it as simple as you can within the needs, and then you work at it until the complexity is mastered.

Q. Does that require players of special intelligence?

A. Well, it takes intelligence to play football at this level, and you take that into account when you select players, of course. But it's still football, and not something more or something less. It's not war and it's not chess. It's football, and you have to grasp its technicalities to work with it successfully.

Q. Is that it? A carefully worked out technical system?

A. Oh, no. That's the starting point. The system also has to be flexible enough to accomodate the particular abilities of the players using it. That's why it's so important that it have a broad base. There may be a whole segment of the offense that's not much use with one kind of player on hand, but very valuable for another kind of player. You have to be able to go back and forth to the appropriate segments according to who's playing—and who the opponent is—without getting outside the boundaries of the whole system that your players and coaches have been learning.

Q. But when sports commentators talk of "philosophy," they always mention more running or more passing, long passes or short passes, defensive alignments. You haven't mentioned any of these things.

A. Well, those are mechanics. And coaches do have different philosophies that lead to certain mechanics. For instance, you can have a philosophy that simply says, "We'll block everybody fiercely and just overpower our opponents, and if we execute that correctly, we can have a very simple plan." That's a perfectly valid approach in some situations, especially for a college team that can rely on having physical superiority over most of its opponents because it usually recruits better than others in its group.

The trouble with that is that it doesn't work the same way in the games where the opponent has equal power. But if you have superiority, it's a good system.

Another team, like the Oakland Raiders traditionally, has a basic idea about throwing long passes to loosen up the defense, and then using straight ahead power. That's obviously been successful for a long time.

Q. What's your basic philosophy then?

A. You'd have to say it's diversity, and good execution of what we call high-percentage plays, plays that minimize risk and take the opportunities a particular defense offers—if they're carried out correctly. And I believe in making a lot of changes, in not falling into a pattern, in not giving the other team the same kind of formation or play to look at it time and again.

Q. How did you arrive at your system?

A. It accumulated over the years, and it's impossible for me to take out a single play now and say, it came from this place or that time. But I was exposed to many fine football minds, from college up.

My ideas about passing are rooted in the year I spent with Oakland back in the middle 1960s. Sid Gillman, from whom Al Davis derived his system, was a true genius in working out the possibilities of passing—and so was Davis. But Gillman is the originator of the modern passing game, and he was doing 29 years ago what has become standard practice only recently. Working there started me on real comprehension of what could be done.

Q. And then? You were at Oakland only one year.

A. That's right, 1966.

Q. What happened?

A. It was a time in my life when I had to reconsider career goals. I decided I'd go back to graduate business school and give up coaching, that it was time to go in another direction.

Q. Did you?

A. I never actually started. This was a time when the National Football League teams were seriously interested in having minor-league farm clubs, and there was such a team in San Jose, and I could coach it part-time, while going to school, so I did that. We had a good team, about 11 players who played in the NFL at one time or another.

Q. But the next season, 1968, you went to Cincinnati as offensive co-ordinator. What changed?

A. It was another career choice, that's all. The Bengals were a new team, just being formed then by Paul Brown, and it looked like the right opportunity to take. So I moved my family to Cincinnati, and it was the right thing to do. We had a very good life there, my children got a fine education, our team had some success.

Q. But when Brown retired as head coach and didn't select you as his successor, did that lead you to second-guess it?

A. No, certainly not. I learned so much from Brown. Just as I learned about passing systems in Oakland, I learned about organizational procedures in Cincinnati.

And I'll tell you what was the greatest thing he did for me. He allowed me to work at home, alone, without being subjected to the committee system. I was the offensive coordinator and I could work with my films, and figure out some cohesive approach, and he would accept it or make some changes, but it was at least a coherent line of thought. And I did that for eight years.

It's very important that there be a single idea behind any system. The usual way, a bunch of coaches sit in a room, and someone at the blackboard says, why don't we try this, and someone who thinks to himself, that's probably not such a hot idea, probably doesn't say it, and suggests a modification instead, and that goes on for hours.

Finally you settle on something that nobody thinks is the best thing because everybody is tired and you have to decide on something.

And even if the plan finally worked out has good things in it, it's a piece of this and a piece of that, with something in it that not everyone understands thoroughly or interprets the same way. So holes pop up, and the one who thought it wasn't such a good idea in the first place grouses about it, and you're wondering who's going to get blamed for what.

Q. Your system, then, really relies on people more than on blueprints?

A. I'd say so. You need good blueprints. But you have to be able to find the right people, and when you do, find the circumstance that lets them do their best work.

Q. Are you going to win Sunday?

A. We expect to play well, and to be prepared, as we have been for most of our games. Winning and losing is often determined by something unexpected and out of your control—a bounce, an official's call, a slip—and you can never account for that until it happens. But we're confident that we're capable of winning, and know what we have to do to succeed, so if the unforseen, exceptional things don't arise, we think we can win the game.

Q. And then?

A. And then I'll have time to think and talk about less immediate things and deeper feelings. And somewhere around April, probably, I'll be fully unwound.

The six main decisions in Walsh's master plan

One can identify six key steps in the transformation of the San Francisco 49ers from just another hopeful "building" team to the one with the best record in the National Football League.

Actually, one could identify 11, or five, or 23, or any other number one felt like choosing. But the arbitrary choice of six makes it possible to tell the story without over-simplification and without excessive detail.

In chronological order, they go this way:

1. The 1981 draft.
2. The signing of Jack Reynolds.
3. The change at left tackle, from Ron Singleton through Ken Bungarda to Dan Audick.
4. The trading away of Steve DeBerg.
5. The acquisition of Johnny Davis for James Owens.
6. The acquisition of Fred Dean.

They have a common thread: Bill Walsh's capacity to act decisively on a conclusion he has reached, even when the decision has obvious dangers.

The drafting of four defensive backs, three of whom have been starters all season and the other a valued reserve, has now been certified as a brilliant stroke. But it required considerable strength of purpose to carry out, and it was greeted with considerable skepticism when it was.

Ronnie Lott was universally recognized as a probable star, but there were no "can't miss" tags on Eric Wright, Carlton Williamson and Lynn Thomas, also chosen in the first five rounds.

And the only other player chosen among them was John Harty, a defensive lineman.

To begin with, this was a dramatic display of confidence in the scouting system and evaluation procedures Walsh had presided over. But it went further. Walsh was clearly identified as an offensive coach, publicly committed to playing "attractive" football, not expected to challenge for any titles quite yet, and painfully aware of his team's offensive needs.

He was fresh out of running backs, with Paul Hofer's physical condition questionable and Earl Cooper's late 1980 performance disappointing, and had only two reliable pass receivers (Fred Solomon and Dwight Clark). If he didn't beef up the offense, and the defense developed only slowly, where would he be?

Any temptation to draft an offensive player after all, despite the master plan to repair the defense, would have been understandable. Some people who worked closely with Walsh, and thought they knew him well (but obviously not as well as they thought), believed he would make such a move at the last minute. But he didn't deviate from the course he had declared.

The next step was daring, too. For two years, the 49ers had a superior passing attack behind a good offensive line, a football team's most tightly knit unit. The left tackle must supply key protection for the right-handed passer's blind side. For two years, Singleton had been the regular left tackle in a successful system.

For whatever reason, Walsh decided Singleton wasn't what he wanted. So he cut him, and installed Bungarda, a converted defensive player with virtually no experience. This was a daring move, and no one knows exactly how it might have worked out. But Bungarda injured his knee during the exhibition season—and the 49ers came up with Audick, an experienced pro, by giving San Diego a future draft choice.

With little attention, Audick has panned out perfectly, playing better than Singleton did. But it took nerve to discard Singleton that way in the first place.

Appreciating Reynolds was easy enough. Negotiating terms, and convincing Reynolds this would be the right place for him, was another study, requiring first-rate executive decision-making.

Walsh had made up his mind about Joe Montana as his quarterback last year, if not earlier. But trading away DeBerg, who had been his first 49er quarterback, on the eve of the new season had a different significance. It strengthened Montana's position, increased the confidence of the other players in Montana, and eliminated any possibility of two-quarterback controversy if Montana did get off to a bad start.

Trading Owens required tough-mindedness, too. Here was the first player Walsh had drafted, his pet project, a prominent college running back who would be converted into a top wide receiver. There are coaches who would be reluctant to admit to themselves, let alone publicly, that the project

Bill Walsh looks at practice

hadn't worked. But Walsh had an opportunity to get an experienced power fullback his team needed, and Owens was the price. He acted.

Dean's importance has been detailed exhaustively, and his falling out with San Diego's management was San Francisco's good luck. But any other team could have dealt for and with him; it was Walsh who found a way to satisfy the player, satisfy the club and keep his own club's salary structure intact.

The sixth step was completed in time for the Oct. 11 game against Dallas. At this point, Walsh's 49ers, over three seasons, were 11-26. Since then they are 13-1.

Chapter 7

Joe Montana

Quarterback Joe Montana is straight out of a middle-American legend, cleft chin, dimples, throwing arm, rows of even teeth and all.

He came to the San Francisco 49ers three seasons ago by way of Notre Dame and a small Pennsylvania town that's hard to pronounce, bringing with him an anglicized Italian name and a laconically even temperament it's hard to believe aren't a put-on.

Known also as Joey (to his mother and Howard Cosell) and Big Sky (to followers of a 1981 newspaper nickname contest that drew 10,000 suggestions), Montana has in the course of the 49ers unexpectedly victorious season become the Bay Area's newest sweetheart. He has become at least vaguely familiar even to people who think that with a last name like that he must be a rodeo champ or an American Indian raised on a reservation.

Joe Montana displays, depending upon the situation, the confidence of a bull or the sweetness of a candystriper. On a football field he displays an intelligence that has helped him achieve one of the best passing records in the National Conference of the National Football League this season. As a result, at the age of 25, he has found himself engaged in a sudden and serious flirtation with fame.

Joe is sitting slouched in a chair at the dining table of his house, tossing a plastic hamburger toy across the room for one of his two miniature dachshunds to retrieve. He throws effortlessly, precisely, from the tips of his fingers, with a controlled flick of the wrist. His hands are big, his fingers long and strong, the nails well-groomed.

It is Wednesday afternoon and he has just left practice, two hours later than scheduled.

He is dressed in a blue warm-up suit, with his wispy blond hair, still damp, curling around the edges of his cap.

Set in his unexpectedly boyish face are eyes the color of the "sky blue" crayons out of a Crayola box. Except for his height and weight (6-foot-2, 200 pounds), the size of his feet (he wears a size 11 boot), and the breadth of his chest (measurement unknown but it appears as solid as a heavy-sand punching bag), Montana probably looks today about the way he did at the age of eight when he started playing midget football in Monongahela, a small farming and mining town just south of Pittsburgh.

An only child, Montana developed with the encouragement of his father, the manager of a branch of a small finance company.

His success, he says, "has been my dad's dream as much as it's been mine."

His father never forced him to play, but, by

paternal decree, once he started a season he had to finish it.

There are plenty of pleasantly ordinary things about Montana: He drives a Chevy truck and a Volkswagen Scirocco, prefers murder mysteries when he reads, has a fetish for electronic games, doesn't care much for country music and takes his rock music hard but not too hard. He calls himself a lapsed—"a real lapsed"—Catholic.

What is success doing to this seemingly unpreposessing fellow? He smiles at the question.

"Nothin'. Really nothin'," he answers with a shrug, stroking his two dogs, Broadway and Bozley, as they clamber over his chest.

It's certainly not making him any chattier.

More people want a piece of Joe Montana's time, that's the biggest change. The stack of fan mail in his locker at the Redwood City training camp had mounted so high by the middle of the season that he gave in and asked the 49ers' public relations department to help him out by addressing and stuffing envelopes.

The fan mail, he maintains, comes mostly from little boys seeking his advice, his autograph or his picture.

"Surprisingly," says his wife, Cass, from the kitchen where she is preparing a pot roast, "there are not very many women who write him." She sounds honestly surprised, and amused.

Joe isn't quite the sex symbol that teammate Dwight Clark is, but he arouses his share of female clamor. That used to bother Cass some but doesn't particularly now that they're married.

Women in the locker room, on the other hand, do bother her, regardless of their intent.

"It's a moral issue to me," she says. "Think of an executive going into his office and taking a shower and having the secretary bringing in a cup of coffee. Wouldn't that be a little weird?"

Before this fall, reporters paid Montana only perfunctory heed. Now they pursue him.

He doesn't mind the attention, it's even flattering. "It's just," he says, "that it's so much so all of a sudden."

Other than the demands on his time, he says, the only difference between Joe Montana, star quarterback, and Joe Montana, rookie, is that his phone rings more often with people asking for tickets. As proof of the negligible effects of success, he notes, "I still have to shovel out the barn."

Actually, Cass Montana shovels out the barn more often than Joe does, at least during football season.

"This six months, all I require of Joe is to play football and I'll take care of the rest," she says, having returned to the den after carting several wheelbarrows full of hay and manure out of the home of their two Arabian horses. Joe has not yet come home from practice and she is left to tend the horses alone.

Cass is 29, four years older than Joe. She is pretty, agile and articulate, unquestionably the more gregarious of the two. She is wearing faded jeans, a plaid cowboy-style shirt, a yellow down vest, a diamond ring and dark red polish on her long fingernails.

She and Joe married this summer after a three-year courtship that started on an airplane. She was the flight attendant when he and the Notre Dame team flew home from a game with the University of Southern California. Notre Dame had lost, but Joe, during the last season game of his college career, had been a hero.

"I got on the plane thinking. 'Oh wow, a bunch of college kids'" she said. "And it *was* a bunch of college kids. I saw this little boy in the back and we struck up a conversation. I had no idea who he was and what had just happened. He didn't bother to tell me and I didn't bother to ask."

They lived together in Los Angeles for a while and moved into a house in the Peninsula hills this summer. Except for its view of undeveloped land that stretches several miles down to the ocean, their three-bedroom home looks like the house of any modestly prosperous young couple. It is filled with contemporary furniture made of light wood or wicker, with lots of plants and macrame and color photographs in metal frames.

What tributes to Joe the house contains are concentrated in this room. On one wall there are two large frames containing pictures of him in uniform and over by the fireplace are a stuffed bear in a red 49ers T-shirt and a painted "game ball" that commemorates the team's surprising 45-14 victory over the Dallas Cowboys in October.

There is one memento in the kitchen, an inverted 49er's helmet turned into a chips-and-dip bowl, a standard team possession. "We use it to collect pennies," Cass says. "I can't see using it for chips. Let's face it, enough's enough."

Enough for Cass might be more than enough for anyone less devoted. She refers to the 49ers as "we," extending the team to include herself and the wives and girlfriends of all the players. She plays on a bowling team with some of the other women and sees a lot of them socially. They are, she says, "the backbones of these fellows."

The tumult and glory of this football season seem not to have thrown the Montana marriage off balance.

"It really hasn't changed our personal lives," Cass says, "He's extremely unassuming. It almost shocks me. I'm thinking come on, you can't be for real sometimes."

But on the field, "quiet, modest" Joe is transformed.

"If he walked out on the field the way he is in real life," she says, "he wouldn't be a leader, he probably wouldn't be playing football. He's got to be cocky out on the field to survive. I don't mean cocky verbally, but confident."

A few minutes later, still waiting for Joe to come home, she pulls out a cigarette, grimacing as she lights it. "He hates this," she says holding up the cigarette and shaking her head in mock disgust. "He's so easy to live with it's sickening. He doesn't drink much, he doesn't smoke. He's neat. Can you imagine a man being neat?"

Every now and then, though, in the middle of some green turf, this virtuous nice guy yells.

"Sometimes I overreact on the field when mistakes are made," he says sitting calmly at the dining table. "Not mistakes really, but somebody does something different from what I read."

For minutes he has been shredding a matchbook, his hands moving all the time. This isn't a sign of nervousness, it seems, but of energy, and except for his hands he is still.

"I get upset at myself," he continues. "Sometimes I yell—not very often—but sometimes I yell at somebody else. I don't like to do that. They get yelled at by the coaches. They don't need another player yelling at them.

"Sometimes I yell when they can't hear me, when they're way down the field." He smiles. "That's better. Sometimes the linemen hear me and they laugh."

Joe admits he hates to be anything less than the best, and he skis, rides horses, plays golf and basketball and competes at electronic games with an intensity that would make you think his livelihood depended upon it.

Before Steve DeBerg—his close friend, former teammate and quarterback rival—was traded this year to the Denver Broncos, the two of them competed in every way they could find. On flights to and from games, he, DeBerg and a couple of other players would spend hours playing cards or backgammon, and the minute they stepped off the plane would go in search of a game room.

Competitive as he is, he is not fearless. He has considered learning to parachute but has yet to get over the worry that his chute wouldn't open.

What about setbacks, he's asked. Surely he's had some.

"A couple," he says. "At Notre Dame."

Now he is drumming his fingers lightly on the the table.

One of them was during his senior year. After sitting out part of his junior year with a separated shoulder, he returned to the team as a senior expecting to be the No. 1 quarterback. He found himself No. 3. "It took me three games to get my position back," he says.

Joe Montana doesn't think a lot about what he will do when the inevitable, if distant, end comes to his football playing career. Something in advertising maybe.

He was a marketing major in college and loves design. The proof, he says, is that he will stand in a grocery store check-out line mesmerized by the colors and lines of cigarette packages. He doubts he has the talent to be a designer himself.

If he says it, he's probably right. He seems to be a man with a keen sense of just what he can learn and just what he has to learn.

"I didn't think I'd develop this fast," he says simply of his success as a professional quarterback. "There are still a lot of things I have to do. I wasn't surprised I'm playing this well, just that it happened this early in my career."

Chapter 8

The Team by Units

Offensive line

One definition of a true football fanatic is someone who can name all the players, and their positions, in the offensive line—without looking at a program.

Take the 49ers' offensive line, an anonymous bunch at best before 1981, their finest of all National Football League seasons.

Any true member of the "49er Faithful" can tell you Randy Cross plays right guard—or is it left guard, or center? Well, the UCLA All-American can play both guard and center, as he did for the Bruins, but he has been a fixture at right guard for the 49ers the past three seasons after playing three years at center.

Cross received recognition of sorts in 1980 when Pro Football Weekly named him to its All-National Football Conference team. This season, as the 49ers surprisingly emerged as the league's winningest team with a 13-3 record, Cross has been getting his due. Opposing players named him to the

Pro Bowl and others have named him All-NFC. He also is the 49ers' Man of the Year because of his efforts for charity causes off the field. Clearly, Cross has arrived in the proper pro football circles.

But what of the other 49er "O" linemen? Can you name them without looking up their numbers?

Right tackle Keith Fahnhorst has been around long enough (eight years), but is still something of a mystery, although he is the 49er player representative and offensive line coach Bobb McKittrick calls him "an accepted leader by the other players on the team."

The others are numbers in the crowd, to most fans. Fred Quillan (No. 56) was good enough at center to move Cross to guard, left guard John Ayers (No. 68) has excellent speed and balance for his size (6-5, 255), and left tackle Dan Audick (No. 61) is one of the quickest tackles in the league. Audick was acquired in a trade from San Diego to replace injured Ken Bungarda, who is expected to compete for a job in 1982.

The backups include veteran Walt Downing at center and guard, second-year man John Choma at tackle and guard, and 6-7 rookie Allan Kennedy from Washington State at tackle.

Offensive backs

It has been carved in newspaper print that a team must have a great running back—well, at least an outstanding one—to succeed in the National Football League.

The 49ers proved the printcarvers wrong in 1981 by compiling the best record (13-3) without benefit of a standout ball carrier.

Most disappointing was Earl Cooper's "sophomore slump" and Paul Hofer's inability to return fully from knee surgery. Consequently, Ricky Patton, who carried once from scrimmage in 1980, led the team in rushing with a modest 543 yards on 152 tries. He scored four touchdowns and his longest run, 28 yards, was the 49ers' longest of the season.

Hofer, sidelined for the National Football Conference playoffs because of the reinjury to his left knee, couldn't practice most of the year and managed only 60 carries for 193 yards and 27 pass receptions for 244 yards.

Although healthy most of the way, Cooper lost the fullback job at times to Johnny Davis and free agent Walt Easley after leading the 49ers in rushing and setting a club receiving record in his promising rookie season. "Coop" finished with 330 rushing yards and a 3.4 average, along with 51 catches for 477 yards.

Cooper provided a hint of optimism late in the season by having his best games against Cincinnati and Houston before being forced out of the finale at New Orleans because of bruised ribs.

Patton's first backup at halfback is Bill Ring, the special teams' specialist from Belmont who rushed for 71 yards on 11 carries against the Saints, by far his best day and second on the club to Patton's 72 yards in the opener at Detroit.

Rookie Amos Lawrence, the No. 3 halfback and

No. 1 kickoff returner with a 25.7 average, is the fastest 49er back, but was used sparingly because of his inexperience and lack of understanding of coach Bill Walsh's involved offense. He carried only 13 times for 48 yards after being acquired from San Diego for a draft choice early in the season.

Davis, a powerful 235-pounder acquired in a trade from Tampa Bay for James Owens early in the season, is a strong blocker and short-yardage runner. He led the team with seven rushing touchdowns while gaining 297 yards on 94 attempts.

Easley, another tough-yardage runner, missed five games because of a sprained knee, but returned against New Orleans. He rushed for 224 yards on 76 carries in his first pro season.

Quarterback Joe Montana is a threat to run, as he did for a 20-yard touchdown against the Giants Nov. 29. He gained 95 yards on 25 tries and scored twice.

Despite their low average gain of 3.5 yards (compared to the opposition's 4.1), the 49ers ran more than they passed in 1981. The situation, as well as their defense, permitted that luxury.

Receivers

Early in the 1981 season, 49er head coach Bill Walsh singled out Freddie Solomon for all-pro consideration and nobody scoffed.

Later in the year, Walsh called Dwight Clark the team's most valuable player and, again, no arguments were voiced.

Walsh was correct—or close to it—in both cases. The trouble is Solomon and Clark play the same position, wide receiver, and only one was likely to receive the credit due both.

Solomon solved the situation by sustaining a succession of late-season injuries. Although his playing time was carefully limited the last four games after the 49ers clinched a post-season playoff berth, Solomon achieved career highs in receptions (59) and receiving yardage (969), and matched his single-season touchdown high by catching eight scoring throws from Joe Montana.

While "Fast Freddie" provided the 49ers with their only notable deep threat, Clark was the catcher in the clutch more often than not. The third-year pro from Clemson set a club record for most catches in a season with 85, and piled up 1,105 yards, the most by a 49er since Gene Washington in 1970.

Clark also broke Solomon's team career record by catching passes in 31 consecutive games, and scored four times, one on a team-leading 78-yarder from Montana.

If the 49ers have a problem at wide receiver, it is a lack of depth, as backups Mike Wilson and Mike Shumann combined for only 12 catches.

Tight end Charle Young enjoyed his best year since his salad days with the Philadelphia Eagles (1973–1975). He caught 37 passes for 400 yards and five touchdowns (second on the team to Solomon) and was voted the Len Eshmont Award for "inspired play" by his teammates.

Fullback Earl Cooper, who set a team record by catching 83 passes as a rookie in 1980, tailed off to 51 receptions as the 49ers elected to throw downfield more. Halfbacks Paul Hofer and Ricky Patton caught 27 apiece, as the 49ers totaled 328 receptions and 3,766 yards to their opponents' 273 for 3,135.

Defensive line

When the 49ers acquired Fred Dean from the San Diego Chargers for future draft considerations Oct. 2, they made one of the shrewdest trades in their history.

Not only did the 49ers obtain a Pro Bowl defensive end for a second-round draft choice and the option to exchange first-round picks in 1983, they gave their improving defense just what it needed—a master pass-rusher.

"Mean" Dean is considered the quickest quarterback sacker in the National Football League by the people who know—the players and coaches. Although he didn't start a game for the 49ers, he led them with 12 sacks and was named to the Pro Bowl for the third time.

Dean's presence meant the 49ers no longer had to blitz linebackers or backs to hurry opposing quarterbacks. They switch from their usual three-four defense to a four-man front when he comes in on passing situations. His constant pressure has helped the 49ers intercept 27 passes and rank among the league's tightest defenses all season.

The 49ers fared surprisingly well while Dean was injured, as ends Lawrence Pillers (seven sacks) and Dwaine Board (six sacks) picked up the slack. The 49ers' "other" starting end in their three-man formation, Jim Stuckey, had 2½ sacks.

Nose tackle Archie Reese, the club's 1980 Len Eshmont Award winner, was credited with only half a sack in 1981, but has been solid at stopping the run.

Reese tied with Pillers and Board for the team lead in most tackles by a defensive lineman (53), while Stuckey made 49 stops.

Rookies John Harty and Pete Kugler have shown promise in reserve roles and appear to figure in the club's future although Kugler wound up on the injured reserve list before the playoffs began.

Harty was drafted in the second round, the 36th player chosen, after earning all Big Ten honors four years in a row at Iowa. Kugler was drafted out of Penn State in the sixth round.

Linebackers

Jack Reynolds likens pro football to war, which should come as no surprise to anyone who watched him play left inside linebacker for the 49ers.

Although Reynolds is a veteran of 12 National Football League seasons and the oldest of the 49ers at 34, he plays with the enthusiasm of a rookie, according to linebacker coach Norb Hecker.

"He's like having a coach on the field," Hecker said. "He's all business. He's always thinking football. He's a great leader by example."

Reynolds, despite coming out of the lineup in most passing situations, is also the 49ers' leading tackler. The former Los Angeles Ram Pro Bowler (in 1976 and 1980) has made 66 solo stops and 51 assists for a total of 117 tackles. Nobody on the club comes close to him (All-National Football Conference cornerback Ronnie Lott is second with 89).

Reynolds, signed as a free agent in June after being waived by the Rams, is flanked on the left side by veteran Willie Harper, who is having his best season in his eighth year out of Nebraska. Harper, like Reynolds, plays primarily in running situations and has made 72 tackles.

Keena Turner, the second-year right outside linebacker from Purdue, is one of the team's most gifted athletes, as his leaping pass interception against Cincinnati demonstrated. Turner is third on the team in tackles with 84 and leads the linebackers in sacks (three for 25 yards in losses) and fumble recoveries (three).

Craig Puki (51 tackles) replaced Dan Bunz (60) as the inside right starter early this season, while Bobby Leopold (65) backs up Turner and fills in wherever needed. Leopold is a leader on the special teams.

Milt McColl, a rookie from Stanford, backs up Harper and intercepted a pass against Washington.

Defensive backs

Here is how the San Francisco 49er defensive backfield—perhaps the biggest surprise, as a unit, in the NFL in 1981—was constructed.

Free safety Dwight Hicks is the veteran of the backfield although this is only his third year in the pros. The former Michigan star came to the 49ers as a free agent in 1979 after failing tryouts with the Detroit Lions in 1978 and Philadelphia Eagles in 1979.

Cornerback Ronnie Lott, the All-American from USC, was the 49ers' first choice in this spring's draft, the eighth player chosen. The other starting cornerback, Eric Wright, was a second-round draft choice this year out of Missouri, the 40th player chosen.

Starting strong safety Carlton Williamson also is a rookie, picked in the third round out of Pittsburgh, the 65th player taken in the draft.

Still another rookie, Lynn Thomas, is the man the 49ers turn to when they use five defensive backs. A college teammate of Williamson at Pitt, Thomas was drafted in the fifth round, the 121st player chosen.

Saladin Martin, who has played extensively as the nickel back also, came to the 49ers as a free agent this season after a tryout with the Jets last year.

Rick Gervais, who played for 49er coach Bill Walsh at Stanford, signed as a rookie free agent before the season and has been cut twice and resigned twice.

Everyone in the National Football League "knows" a team cannot win playing rookies at cornerback.

Everyone, that is, but Bill Walsh and his defensive assistant coaches on the 49ers. They knew they had the worst secondary in the league in 1979 and 1980 when they finished 2-14 and 6-10, so they drafted three defensive backs in the first three rounds of the draft.

Having drafted them, Walsh and his staff went ahead and played them, reasoning it is wiser to go with inexperienced talent than untalented experience. So-called experts shrugged and said, "No way they can win playing three rookies back there."

But the 49ers did just that, compiling the best record (13-3) in the league and making the playoffs for the first time since 1972. The rookie backs? They not only survived—they thrived.

Ronnie Lott, of course, has been the key figure in the secondary all season, along with the sole holdover, free safety Dwight Hicks, a third-year free agent from Michigan. Both were voted to the National Football Conference Pro Bowl team by their peers, and Lott made Sports Illustrated's All-NFL club.

Ironically, neither Lott nor right sidekick Eric Wright from Missouri played cornerback in college. Both were safeties, but Walsh figured they had the athletic ability to switch.

Walsh said Lott, a two-year All-American at USC, "just may be the best athlete we have" upon drafting him in the first round.

Lott, a 6-foot, 200-pound stinging tackler, proved Walsh right in a hurry. He intercepted seven passes and returned three for touchdowns to set a 49er record, forced four fumbles, recovered two and finished second to linebacker Jack Reynolds in tackles with 89.

The ultimate compliment was paid Lott late in the season when opposing teams deliberately passed away from him. They didn't find Wright much softer, as he led the club in passes defensed (24), intercepted three, recovered two fumbles and forced a fumble to set up the clinching touchdown against Houston.

The third rookie, Carlton Williamson, plays strong safety like Jack Tatum used to for the Oakland Raiders. Williamson is a fierce hitter who intercepted four passes, caused a fumble and recovered two others. Like Lott, he made the United Press International All-Rookie team.

Hicks was the team leader in interceptions as well as experience with nine thefts. He also recovered two fumbles, including one for an 80-yard touchdown return against Washington, and caused one.

Special teams

The man the 49ers call "Mo" missed four games with a hip-pointer at the start of this season, but was easily the team's most valuable special teams' player.

And, no, "Larry" and "Curly" didn't figure, although Lawrence Pillers certainly had his moments in the defensive line.

"Mo" is short for "Mohair," which is what the 49ers call Ray Wersching because, as injured running back Paul Hofer observed, "He has more hair on his body than any guy on the team."

Wersching, a nine-year veteran from the University of California completing his fifth consecutive standout season for the 49ers, is better known for kicking field goals and extra points.

Statistically, 1981 was an off season for Wersching, by his standards. He tied a club record he shares with several others by making all 30 of his extra points, but made "only" 17 of 23 field-goal attempts.

While nobody has heard head coach Bill Walsh complain about Wersching's 74 percent field-goal accuracy, it is slightly below his 1979 (20 of 24) and 1980 (15 of 19) efforts.

Wersching, however, earned his salary by making a 37-yarder on the last play of the game to give the 49ers a 33-31 victory over the Rams in Los Angeles Nov. 22.

It should be noted that Wersching, who made all nine field-goal tries under 30 yards, has to do approximately half his kicking at Candlestick Park, which usually offers the loosest grass surface in the league.

Candlestick also presents swirling wind problems for punters, but barefoot booter Jim Miller set a 49er record by punting for 3,858 yards in 1981, his second National Football League season. Miller averaged 41.5 yards per punt, the highest by a 49er since Tom Wittum's 41.9 in 1975.

Not all of Miller's efforts were boomers, and the 49ers' punt coverage left more than a little to be desired. The Niners ranked 27th among the 28 NFL teams in opposition punt-return average and last in net punting average (though eighth in gross punt average).

They didn't do much better in returning punts, ranking 22nd despite having a pair of breakaway threats in Freddie Solomon and Dwight Hicks.

The 49ers fared better in returning kickoffs. Rookie Amos Lawrence was second in the National Football Conference and third in the league with a 25.7 average, highlighted by a 92-yarder for a touchdown in Los Angeles. Bill Ring was next with a respectable 21.7 average.

Lawrence fumbled away two kickoffs in the season finale at New Orleans and in the Super Bowl.

The 49ers were 16th in kickoff return coverage, with Lawrence, Ring and Bobby Leopold leading the tacklers. All-NFC guard Randy Cross accurately snaps for punts and placements, and quarterback Joe Montana is a sure-handed holder.

Quarterbacks

At the start of the 1981 season, Joe Montana was backing up Steve DeBerg at quarterback for the 49ers.

After the Super Bowl, Montana directed the National Football Conference offense against the AFC in the Pro Bowl.

Obviously, Montana has come a long way in a short time. He replaced DeBerg (now with the Denver Broncos) late last season and set a 49er record by completing 64.5 percent of his passes.

Montana, a third-year player from Notre Dame, completed 63.7 percent in 1981 to lead the NFC in quarterback proficiency rating (88.2). For the second consecutive year, he threw for more touchdowns (19) than interceptions (12) and came within 87 yards of DeBerg's passing-yardage record set in 1979.

For keepers of records, Montana completed 311 of 488 passes for 3,565 yards. His quick feet enabled him to escape all but 26 sacks, compared to the 36 recorded by the 49er defense. He also ran for 95 yards and two touchdowns in 1981 despite being slowed by a sprained ankle and bruised ribs.

While Montana is considered modest and shy off the field, his performances at Candlestick Park have made him a favorite among the fans, inspiring a Bay Area newspaper to run a Montana nickname contest. Joe was asked to choose the winning name and selected "Big Sky," a name that never caught on. An alternative would be "Sourdough Joe."

Former Stanford University All-American Guy Benjamin is Montana's backup. He was seldom called on by coach Bill Walsh until the 49ers clinched their first NFC West title and playoff berth since 1972.

Benjamin lacks Montana's mobility, but "has been throwing beautifully all season," according to the man who counts, Walsh. Benjamin completed 15 of 26 passes for 171 yards and one touchdown.

Paul Hofer

Paul Hofer did not play in the Super Bowl game. He won't play any more football at all. The injured knee that interrupted his career in the sixth game of the 1980 season was re-injured in the 15th game of 1981, and he announced his retirement during Super Bowl week. But his contributions to the 49er success story were fundamental, and not forgotten. He succeeded O.J. Simpson as the starting halfback

Paul Hofer

during 1979, and was the ideal runner-receiver for Walsh's system. As an 11th round draft choice in 1976, he was used little for three years under four head coaches, but blossomed into true stardom under Walsh. His teammates voted him the team's Len Eshmont Award, as their most inspirational player, two years in a row, 1978 and 1979, an honor no other 49er has achieved. And it was Hofer who made possible the fast start in 1980, before he was hurt, and who helped significantly in several key victories in 1981. His record:

Hofer's career

RUSHING

Year	G	Att	Yds	Avg	LG	TD
1976	14	18	74	4.1	17	0
1977	14	34	106	3.1	10	0
1978	16	121	465	3.8	40	7
1979	15	123	615	5.0	47	7
1980	6	60	293	4.9	26	1
1981	12	60	193	3.2	12	1
CAREER	77	416	1746	4.2	47	16

RECEIVING

Year	G	No	Yds	Avg	LG	TD
1976	14	4	45	11.3	13	1
1977	14	5	46	9.2	16	0
1978	16	12	170	14.2	46	0
1979	15	58	662	11.4	44	2
1980	6	41	467	11.4	28	2
1981	6	27	244	9.0	22	0
CAREER	77	147	1634	11.1	46	5

Hofer's record, game-by-game

1980

Opponent	Rushing	Receiving	TDs	Result
New Orleans	12–68	7–114	1	W, 22–23
St. Louis	14–89	9–135	2	W, 24–21
New York Jets	10–40	6–79	0	W, 37–27
Atlanta	14–57	10–48	0	L, 17–20
Los Angeles	9–34	9–91	0	L, 26–48
Dallas*	1–5	0–0	0	L, 14–59
TOTALS	60–293	41–467	3	

*Injured in first quarter

1981

Opponent	Rushing	Receiving	TDs	Result
Atlanta	0–0	1–22	0	L, 17–34
New Orleans	4–19	2–7	0	W, 21–14
Dallas	11–40	3–22	1	W, 45–14
Green Bay	8–3	5–44	0	W, 13–3
Los Angeles	8–23	0–0	0	W, 20–17
Pittsburgh	5–26	1–2	0	W, 17–14
Atlanta	1–0	1–21	0	W, 17–14
Cleveland	10–33	7–64	0	L, 12–15
Los Angeles	5–16	2–20	0	W, 33–31
New York Giants	8–33	4–31	0	W, 17–10
Houston	0–0	1–11	0	W, 28–6
TOTALS	60–193	27–244	1	

Nicknames

When Jack Reynolds came to the San Francisco 49ers this June, he was known as "Hacksaw."

It seems that Reynolds, a standout inside linebacker for the Los Angeles Rams for 11 seasons, earned that nickname by sawing his 1953 Chevy in half after his college football team, Tennessee, lost to Mississippi.

Reynolds has been given a new nickname since joining the 49ers. Some of the players, inspired by champion nickname-giver Paul Hofer, refer to him as "Cheapsaw."

Why?

"Because he'll steal anything in the dressing room," 49er co-trainer Hal Wyatt said after practice one day. "He takes towels, socks, anything he can get his hands on."

The 33-year-old Reynolds has developed followers on the 49ers. Wyatt said Craig Puki, a young linebacker from Tennessee, is sometimes called "Jigsaw" because "he shadows Reynolds all the time."

Linebacker coach Norb Hecker suggested the 49ers' other inside linebacker, Dan Bunz, should be called "Buzzsaw." That would give the 49ers "Hacksaw," (or "Cheapsaw"), "Jigsaw" and "Buzzsaw" protecting the middle.

Wyatt, dubbed "Squirrel" and "Peanut" by Hofer, reminded Hecker that Bunz already is called "Horse" or "Horse Head" because certain players think he looks like one. Bunz used to be called "Amy," because of a supposed likeness to Amy Carter, but that name disappeared when President Jimmy Carter was voted out of office.

Hofer, the quick-quipping running back, has been shackled with some nasty nicknames in his six years with the 49ers. "They used to call him 'Scrub' because he scrubbed for O. J. Simpson back in the Joe Thomas days," Wyatt said. "They also called him 'Joe' after Joe Thomas. Now it's

'Scum Bag' or 'Dirt Bag.'"

Why?

"He knows why," Wyatt said. Hofer laughed and walked out of the trainer's room.

Hofer has laid some memorable monikers on his teammates. He stuck linebacker Bobby Leopold with "Plum Head" and "Onion Head" and running back Lenvil Elliott with "Rat Daddy." Now Elliott is simply called "Rat."

Lindsy McLean, the 49er's other co-trainer, reminded Wyatt that injured running back Phil Francis, a Stanford man, is known as "Filthy" for obvious reasons. "He's always dirty," McLean confided. Francis won back-to-back "worst dresser" contests as a senior at Stanford and as a 49er rookie.

Massive offensive tackle Ken Bungarda, sidelined for the season by knee surgery, has been called "Tarzan" since his college days at Missouri. Asked why, Bungarda replied, "I guess because I kind of look like him." Nobody argued with the 6-foot-6, 270-pounder who has his auto license plates inscribed "Tarzan-1."

Defensive end Dwaine Board is called "Pee-Wee" because he isn't. The name would better suit nose guard Archie Reese, who undoubtedly has inspired something more original from Hofer. Not all of the nicknames are fit to print in a family newspaper, it should be noted.

Offensive guard John Ayers has been known to answer to "Pinocchio," while linebacker Willie Harper is sometimes referred to as "Mouth" because of the size of his. Nobody would like to be called "Mouth," but what would one make of "Five Head," as Elliott is sometimes called?

Fred Solomon has been crowned "Fast Freddie" by the media. What else should a guy who can run the 40 in 4.3 be called? How about "Casper," which Solomon was called when he played for the Miami Dolphins?

Place-kicker Ray Wersching has been named "Mohair" because he has more hair on his body than anybody on the team, while wide receiver Mike Shumann is "Shudog," an obvious play on his name. Others of that nature include Famous Amos Lawrence and Mean Fred Dean.

Many players are called by their initials or shortened forms of their name. Tight end Charle Young is "Cy," running back Bill Ring is "Ringer," defensive end Jim Stuckey is "Stuck," wide receiver Dwight Clark is "DC" and Earl Cooper is "Coop."

Others try to escape that mold. Defensive back Ricky Churchman, called "Churchy," has a poster of John Belushi attached to his dressing cubicle with "Samurai Ricky" scribbled across it.

Some players, such as quarterback Joe Montana, seem to escape the ritual, although Montana reputedly "hates" to be called "Joey" on national television by ABC's Howard Cosell.

Other nicknames are perfectly suited to their subject, such as "Hacksaw" Reynolds and Ronnie "Lott-a-Money" Lott, the 49ers' high-salaried No. 1 draft choice.

Chapter 9

The Coaches

CHUCK STUDLEY, Defensive Coordinator

Chuck Studley's third season as the 49ers' defensive coordinator was his 13th year in the NFL, after spending ten seasons with the Cincinnati Bengals, where he coached for Paul Brown and Bill Johnson.

Chuck was a successful college coach before entering the pro ranks. He won two Missouri Valley Conference championships as head coach at the University of Cincinnati (1961–68). He also coached the University of Massachusetts to a Yankee Conference title in 1960, before beginning an 18-year association with Cincinnati.

An All-America guard at Illinois, Studley was captain of the 1951 Illini Rose Bowl team that captured the Big 10 title with a 9—0—1 record. After graduation, he spent three years coaching at Alton High School in Illinois, before he joined the University of Illinois staff (1955–60).

NORB HECKER, Linebackers

Norb Hecker, the 49ers' linebackers coach, returned to the pro ranks in 1979 following seven years at Stanford University, the last two coaching on Bill Walsh's staff there.

As a player, Norb was a Little All-America offensive end at Baldwin-Wallace College in northeastern Ohio. His professional career began with the Los Angeles Rams, where he played both offensive end and defensive back (1951–53). He then went to Toronto of the Candian Football League in 1954, then to the Washington Redskins a year later.

He returned to the CFL as a player-coach in 1958 with the Hamilton Tiger Cats. In 1959, Hecker joined Vince Lombardi as an assistant coach in Green Bay. With the Packers he was part of the team's glory years in the 1960s and has three World Championship rings from his time there. He has a fourth championship ring from his Rams playing days.

Hecker, co-founder of the NFL Players Association, left Green Bay in 1966 to become the first head coach of the Atlanta Falcons, a post he held for two and one-half years.

His final pro stint before going to Stanford in 1972 was three years (1969–71) as defensive coordinator for the New York Giants.

GEORGE SEIFERT, Defensive Backs

New to the 49er coaching staff in 1980 was George Seifert, the secondary coach. Seifert was regarded as one of the nation's top tutors of defensive backs following 15 years in the collegiate ranks, six of those years at Stanford University, when he was asked to join the 49ers.

After graduation from Utah in 1963, Seifert served a six-month tour of duty with the U.S. Army before returning to Utah as a graduate assistant coach. Then, in 1965, he was named head coach at Westminster College in Salt Lake City.

He moved on to Iowa (1966), then Oregon (1967–71) as an assistant there before joining the Stanford staff (1972–74) as secondary coach, transforming the defensive backfield into the Pac-8 Conference's best statistically in both '72 and '73.

Seifert left Stanford in 1975 to become head coach at Cornell University. He returned to Stanford to join Bill Walsh's coaching staff in 1977. The Cardinals were second in pass defense in the Pac-10 in both '78 and '79. He is a native San Franciscan.

SAM WYCHE, Quarterbacks

Sam Wyche was a walk-on quarterback at Furman University in 1962. After college he signed and played one year for the Wheeling Ironmen of the Continental Football League in Wheeling, West Virginia. The following year was spent as a graduate assistant for Paul Dietzel at the University of South Carolina, where he also obtained his master's degree in Business Administration.

Wyche then played nine years in the NFL, beginning with the expansion Cincinnati Bengals in

1968. He was traded to the Washington Redskins (1971–73), then to Detroit (1974–75). Sam played with St. Louis and Buffalo his final season in 1976.

Wyche gathered football knowledge playing for George Allen, Don Coryell, Jack Pardee, Ted Marchibroda, Paul Brown, Paul Dietzel and Raymond Berry in addition to Bill Walsh in Cincinnati.

BOBB McKITTRICK, Offensive Line

Bobb McKittrick has been an NFL coach since 1971, nearly all of that time under Tommy Prothro. His 20-year association with Prothro began with three years (1955–57) as a Prothro-coached player at Oregon State. He joined the coaching staff at Oregon State in 1961 after three years as a Marine Corps officer, and then went to UCLA (1965–70) as an assistant coach with Prothro.

They later went on to the Los Angeles Rams (1971–72), before once again moving, this time to the San Diego Chargers.

Bobb took a sabbatical from football in 1973 to do graduate work at his alma mater before rejoining Prothro at San Diego. He also coached there under Don Coryell at the conclusion of the 1978 season.

BILL McPHERSON, Defensive Line

After spending one season as the 49ers' linebacker coach (1979), Bill McPherson directed the 49ers' defensive line in 1980. A defensive tackle at Santa Clara in the early '50s, McPherson began coaching in 1956 at his high school alma mater, San Jose's Bellarmine Prep (1956–62), following Army service in Korea. He later was the defensive coordinator at Santa Clara (1963-74) for 12 years before moving to UCLA (1975-77). McPherson coached defensive lines at both Santa Clara and UCLA.

At UCLA, McPherson worked with Dick Vermeil. He later joined Vermeil's Philadelphia Eagles' staff as linebackers coach in 1978, before moving back to his native state of California with the 49ers.

MILT JACKSON, Special Teams—Receivers

Milt Jackson, the 49ers' special teams-receivers coach, was a four-sport athlete at Sacramento's Grant High School in football, basketball, track and baseball in the 1960s. After a football-baseball collegiate career at Tulsa, he was drafted by both the 49ers (sixth round) and Philadelphia Phillies (first round) in 1967. He was a cornerback in football and a pitcher in baseball.

Prior to coming to San Francisco, Jackson spent five years coaching in the Pacific-10 Conference. He coached UCLA's offensive tackles and tight ends in 1979 after coming from the University of Oregon (1977-78), where he had been the defensive backfield coach.

BILLIE MATTHEWS, Running Backs

Billie Matthews joined the 49ers staff in 1979 after spending eight seasons at UCLA (1971-78). Included among the UCLA runners Matthews directed were five 1,000-yard rushers: Kermit Johnson, James McAlister, Wendell Tyler and Theotis

Brown (twice). The '73 Bruin squad rushed to 4,403 yards in 11 games.

Billie also spent a season at Kansas (1970) where he coached current pro backs John Riggins and Delvin Williams.

AL VERMEIL, Conditioning

The 49ers' strength and conditioning programs again were directed by Al Vermeil.

A well-known Bay Area coach at the prep level for a number of years, Vermeil was head football coach and athletic director at Moreau High School in Hayward, California, for six years (1973–78). His teams won two championships and one co-championship during the period. Vermeil was named Coach of the Year in 1975 in the Catholic Athletic League, a Bay Area prep league.

CAS BANASZEK, Assistant Offensive Line

Casimir Joseph Banaszek, II, known as Cas to his teammates during his nine playing years with the San Francisco 49ers, has returned to the Niners, this time as an assistant to Offensive Line Coach Bobb McKittrick. With the appointment, he becomes the tenth member of Bill Walsh's coaching staff.

A Chicago native and a graduate of Northwestern (1967), Banaszek was the offensive line coach at the University of California in 1979 and 1980. His playing career ended abruptly when he suffered a broken leg in the sixth game of the 49ers' 1977 season.

Chapter 10

And a Cast of Thousands

The 49er organization

Management
EDWARD J. DeBARTOLO, Jr. ....President
FRANKLIN MIEULI. .... Limited Partner
MRS. VICTOR P. MORABITO .... Limited Partner

Administrative Staff

JOHN McVAY .... Director of Football Operations
KEN FLOWER ...... Director of Marketing & Community Affairs
KEITH SIMON. .... Business Manager
GEORGE HEDDLESTON .... Director of Public Relations
JERRY WALKER......... Assistant Director of Public Relations
DELIA NEWLAND .... Assistant Director of Publicity
TED GLARROW .... Ticket Manager
KEN DARGEL .... Assistant Ticket Manager
R.C. OWENS .... Executive Assistant
MELRENE FREAR .... Controller
ROY GILBERT. .... Film Director
WALT POREP .... Game Films Photographer
MICHAEL ZAGARIS,
DENNIS DESPROIS .... Photographers
MICHAEL OLMSTEAD .... Entertainment Director
CHRIS POEHLER,
PAUL POTYEN .... Band Directors
S. DAN BRODIE. .... Statistician
CHICO NORTON .... Equipment Manager
DON KLEIN,
WAYNE WALKER .... 49ers' Radio
GREG COSMOS,
TED WALSH .... Assistant Equipment Managers

[128]

Medical Staff

LINDSY McLEAN,
HAL WYATT ....Co-Trainers
FRED L. BEHLING, M.D.,
JAMES B. KLINT, M.D......................Team Physicians

Scouting Staff

TONY RAZZANO .... Director of College Scouting
PROVERB JACOBS......................... Pro Scouting
VIC LINDSKOG ....Scout
ERNIE PLANK......................................Scout
WARREN SCHMAKEL.................................Scout
NEIL SCHMIDT.....................................Scout
BILLY WILSON.....................................Scout
NEAL DAHLEN............................. Staff Assistant

Coaching Staff

BILL WALSH................. General Manager-Head Coach
CHUCK STUDLEY .... Defensive Coordinator
NORB HECKER .... Linebackers
MILT JACKSON .... Special Teams—Receivers
BILLIE MATTHEWS .... Running Backs
BOBB McKITTRICK........................ Offensive Line
BILL McPHERSON.........................Defensive Line
GEORGE SEIFERT............................... Secondary
AL VERMEIL .... Strength and Conditioning
SAM WYCHE...............................Quarterbacks
CAS BANASZEK .... Assistant Offensive Line
RAY RHODES........................Assistant Secondary

Office Staff

RICK MORABITO.............................Ticket Office
DAWNA ALLEN ....Payroll/Insurance
LYNN CARROZZI...........................Ticket Office
PAULETTE ELLIOTT ....College Scouting
DOTTIE HERKEN .... Defensive Coaches
HILARY HEUERMANN .... Football Operations
NICOLE LANGERAK.......... Head Coach/General Manager
                         Offensive Coaches/Special Teams
ANGE REPETTO............................... Bookkeeping
DOLORES RIGAS ....Ticket Office
LINDA SAUNDERS .... Marketing/Community Affairs
WINNIE TORO ....Business Office
MIDGE WILLIAMS .... Receptionist/Fan Mail & Films

In today's era of specialists, the San Francisco 49ers have two who direct the front office portion of the team's day-to-day operation—Director of Football Operations John McVay and Director of Marketing and Community Affairs Ken Flower.

JOHN McVAY,
Director of Football Operations

John McVay specializes in all front office aspects pertaining to football, specifically pro and college scouting and drafting, player contract negotiations, trades and waivers.

Prior to 1981, McVay was the 49ers' Director of Player Personnel for two seasons, and thus responsible for preparing the 49ers drafting strategy. He also supervised the organization's scouting department and is continuing to oversee those areas of the 49ers' operation in his new role. He assumes many of the duties of a general manager for 49ers' Coach-GM Bill Walsh during the football season, when Walsh's attentions must be focused more on the coaching half of his dual role.

A former college and pro head coach himself and also a one-time college athletic director, McVay has four decades of football experience at every level to draw from. Prior to joining the 49ers in early 1979, he was the head coach of the New York Giants for one-and-a-half years.

He originally went to the Giants in late 1975 as an assistant coach in charge of research and development but was elevated by Owner Wellington Mara to replace fired Head coach Bill Arnsparger at the midway point of the '76 season. McVay's record with the giants was 14-23.

Prior to joining the Giants, he was the head coach and general manager of the Memphis Southmen of the World Football League, where his team won 24 of 31 games in the year and one-half that league existed. McVay had left the University of Dayton, where he was head football coach for nine years (1965–73) and athletic director in 1972 and '73, to join the Southmen.

An Ohio native from famed Massillon High School, McVay played collegiately at Miami of Ohio for Woody Hayes and Ara Parseghian. A three-year starter at center, he won All-Midwest and team MVP honors his final two years. He went from there to become one of Miami's 20-plus "Cradle of Coaches" alumni who are successful football coaches and administrators at the college and pro levels.

KEN FLOWER, Director of Marketing and Community Affairs

Ken Flower scrutinizes all matters relating to radio and television broadcasting, along with directing all advertising and marketing sales. He also oversees business affairs with the city of San Francisco and at Candlestick Park.

Flower moved into his job full-time last season after spending the previous year in a consulting role with the 49ers' staff.

A native son of San Francisco and one of the finest West Coast basketball players in history, Flower has an extensive background in sales and marketing, including other jobs connected to the National Football League with NFL Films and at CBS and ABC.

In addition to his various administrative responsibilities, Flower handles the 49ers' broadcasting relations with local radio and television, and coordinates all business affairs with the city and county of San Francisco for 49ers' operations at Candlestick Park.

A graduate of Lowell High School in San Francisco and Menlo College, he obtained his BA degree from Southern California in 1954. As a roundballer at USC, he was the Southern California Collegiate Player of the Year in 1953–54, his team's captain, All-Pacific Coast Conference and an All-America selection.

Following graduation, he entered the U.S. Air Force as a First Lieutenant and coached the U.S. Air Force All-Star basketball team to the AAU National Championship in 1957.

LINDSY McLEAN, Co-Trainer

Lindsy McLean has been a trainer for 19 years, including 11 years as head trainer at the University of Michigan prior to joining the 49ers as co-trainer in 1979.

Before he became Michigan's trainer, McLean served three years as head trainer at San Jose State University (1965–67) and two years as head trainer at the University of California at Santa Barbara (1963–64).

A native of Nashville and a 1960 graduate of Vanderbilt, McLean received his certification in physical therapy from Herman Hospital in Houston in 1961.

HAL WYATT, Co-Trainer

Hal Wyatt was in his fourth season as co-trainer in 1981, after serving the Niners as assistant trainer in 1977 and 1978.

Wyatt is a native Texan from San Angelo who graduated from North Texas State University with a degree in physical education in 1972. Hal spent the next three years operating a sports medicine clinic in Dallas, where he was trainer for the Dallas Tornado soccer team in 1975. He joined the 49ers in July '77.

CHICO NORTON, Equipment Manager

Forrest "Chico" Norton has become a virtual San Francisco 49ers institution. Chico, whose nickname comes from his hometown of Chico, California, begins his 27th year as 49ers' equipment manager. He has been with the organization longer than any other working member.

Born November 24, 1919, Norton first entered professional athletics when he went to work for the San Francisco Seals baseball team in 1948. He joined the 49ers in 1955.

Wives

Susie Fahnhorst, Laurel Ayers and Patrice Cross know what is involved in being married to a man on a struggling professional football team.

In 1981, the wives of starting San Francisco 49er offensive linemen Keith Fahnhorst, John Ayers and Randy Cross discovered what it's like being married to a champion.

The difference is surprising.

Susie Fahnhorst thought winning would make things easier at home in San Carlos, but she has found out the opposite.

"Keith definitely is harder to live with," Suzie, a Minnesota native, said. "The pressure is never off. When we used to lose so much, we would get into a pattern of depression. But when you win, we have found out the pressure is always on."

"John is more intense and the pressure is greater," Laurel Ayers said from her in-season home in San Carlos. "John is like me: It's hard for us to believe what is happening. I just hope the bubble doesn't burst."

Susie Fahnhorst almost missed the most exciting season in her husband's eight-year career.

"To be perfectly honest, Keith is a real crab to live with during the football season," she said. "I told Keith before the season started I really wanted to stay in St. Paul. But he told me the other day the reason he wanted me to come out was he did not expect this much success this year, and he thought he would need somebody's shoulder to cry on.

"As it turned out, there are all these 'groupie' women hanging around; he was kidding me, saying he wished I would have stayed home.

"Now I'm happy I came."

The Fahnhorsts live in St. Paul during the off-season with their two children, Tiffany (2½) and Britt (6 months), and have no plans on becoming Californians.

"We think Minnesota is a better place to rear children," Susie said. "Out here, the pace is just so fast. Back home, we live in the woods; we think it is a nice place for our children to grow up."

And Susie definitely feels more at home in St. Paul.

"To be perfectly honest, the team's success has made me a little more insecure within myself. I feel at times that I have not had a chance to pursue my career. I really would like to open up a cookie shop or something. I have some great recipes. And these groupies make me feel like I'm not good enough—sometimes."

Laurel Ayers, meanwhile, is not going to let the 49ers' success bother her a bit.

"I am a rather simple person to begin with," she said with an eye on her 2½-year-old son, J.T., who looks like a prototype of his father. "People didn't know who I was before, and I like it that way. I prefer anonymity. I'm lucky, I don't have to play up to the adoring public."

But some 49er wives are not that lucky.

"I really have sympathy for Cass Montana," Laurel said in her Texas accent. "Those people (from the television stations) are at her house shooting film of her and Joe's lifestyle.

"At least there's no threat on John's life. The person would have to be a fool," she said, making a light-hearted reference to a threat on 49er quarterback Joe Montana's life late in the season.

"I am a very shy person," Laurel said. "One of the local television stations did a thing on the 49er wives. When the cameras went on, I hid.

"I think this season is a great reward for those players who suffered through those 2-14 seasons. It's amazing how many more friends you have.

"Some of the real heroes are the fans. Can you imagine waiting in line on Christmas Day to buy tickets? Everyone is so thrilled. John doesn't want to let anybody down. He has a real healthy attitude."

What is it like to be a 49er wife?

"It's like one big happy family, and we are the kids," Patrice Cross said.

Patrice and Randy know about big, happy families. "I have five sisters and a brother, and Randy has five sisters and a brother.

"There's never a dull moment, and very little time to put your legs up and relax," she said. "Randy would love to cash in while he can. You have to think about the future. What's going to happen when it (football) is over? It's like taking a kid out of a candy store. We hope for other things after football."

Patrice has found life at home closer to normal than the other wives interviewed, partly because the Crosses live in Redwood City year-around.

"He's been in a much better mood this season," Patrice said. "He's much easier to get along with. But Randy never causes friction."

Just as Randy has his role with the 49ers, Patrice has one at home.

"My job is to be supportive. To be the one at home. I like everybody, but basically I stay by myself. Being the wife of a pro athlete has its ups and downs. It's been exciting this year. We're on cloud nine."

Patrice saves much of her excitement for game days.

"I'm more of a passive type," she said, "but when I go to the games, I'm a rah-rah, gung-ho type. I want to know what's going on.

"I used to say I was the mother hen with the new players' wives. I always would introduce myself and say, 'I'll be your friend.' This is the first year I have bowed out of that role. It is hard meeting people and then seeing them go, either getting cut or traded.

"I'm not a party-hearty this year," Patrice said. "We're staying home, getting lots of rest. I guess when you're a winner, that's how it is."

Chapter 11

The Super Bowl Game

SUPER BOWL XVI
SAN FRANCISCO 49ERs (NFC) vs. CINCINNATI BENGALS (AFC)
Pontiac Silverdome, Pontiac, Michigan
Sunday, January 24, 1982

San Francisco won the toss and elected to **receive**. *Cincinnati* chose to defend the **north** goal.

First quarter: The kickoff came at 4:20 PM EST from Breech to the 49er 27, where it went out of bounds for a five-yard **penalty** to Cincinnati. Breech's next kickoff went from his 30 to Lawrence on his nine and he returned 17 yards, fumbled and Simmons recovered for the Bengals on the 49er 26.

BENGALS

1/10/S26	14:46	Anderson passed complete to Curtis for eight yards (Reynolds) (4R-4P).
2/2/S18		Johnson hit center for two yards and a **first down** (Reese).
1/10/S16		Anderson passed complete to Ross at the 14 and he ran to the five for a gain of 11 and **first down** (Reynolds).
1/5/S5		Alexander tried left tackle and made nothing (Harper).
2/5/S5		Anderson was sacked for a passing loss of five yards (Stuckey). Make it minus six.
3/11/S11		Anderson's pass for Curtis was intercepted by Hicks on his five and he returned 27 yards to his 32 (Wilson forced him out of bounds).

49ERS

1/10/S32	11:50	Montana's screen pass left was good to Patton for six yards (Edwards).
2/4/S38		Montana passed complete to Clark for six yards, **first down** (Harris).
1/10/S44		Cooper tried to circle left end and made nothing (Browner).
2/10/S44		Montana passed complete to Solomon for nine yards (Kemp).
3/1/C47		Patton ran right, handed off to Solomon coming right to left, Solomon lateralled back to Montana who passed complete to Young for 14 yards, **first down** (LeClair).
1/10/C33		Montana's pass meant for Ramson was dropped by Breeden of Cincinnati, incomplete.
2/10/C33		Cooper drove inside right end for 11 yards and a **first down** (Kemp).
1/10/C22		Ring raced inside right end for seven yards (Breeden).
2/3/C15		Cooper ran wide around left end and was stopped for no gain (Riley).
3/3/C15		Montana passed complete to Solomon on the five and he ran to the one for a gain of 14 yards and a **first down** (Breeden).
1/1/C1		***Montana dived high over center and right guard into the end zone for a one-yard touchdown and a first down.***

Wersching, with Montana holding, converted.

S.F. 7   CIN 0   DRIVE: 68 YDs, 11 P (9:08)

Wersching kicked off for San Francisco to Verser on his five and he returned 14 (Gervais).

BENGALS

1/10/C19	5:43	Anderson passed complete to Johnson for a gain of three yards (Leopold).
2/7/C22		Anderson passed complete to Johnson in the right flat for five yards (Lott).
3/2/C27		Anderson bootlegged around right end for three yards, **first down** (ran out of bounds)
1/10/C30		Johnson drove inside right guard for three yards (Reese).
2/7/C33		Anderson ran from pass formation around left end for six yards (Wright).
3/1/C39		Johnson ran over right guard for two yards and a **first down** (Reynolds).

1/10/C41 Anderson's long pass meant for Collinsworth was broken up by Wright at the 15.
2/10/C41 Anderson's pass was caught out of bounds by Collinsworth at the 45, incomplete.
3/10/C41 Anderson was sacked for a passing loss of four yards (Turner).
4/14/C37 McInally punted 53 yards to San Francisco ten where it was downed.

49ERS
1/10/S10 1:01 Montana's pass meant for Clark was broken up by Riley.
2/10/S10 Patton tried left end and was dropped for a loss of seven yards (Browner).
3/17/S3 Cincinnati **penalty,** five yards, 12 men on the field (illegal procedure).
3/12/S8 Patton ran around right end for four yards (Browner) as the quarter ended.

FIRST QUARTER SCORE: S.F. 7   CIN 0

	S.F.	CIN
First downs	5	4
Net yards rush	16	16
Net yards pass	49	17
Att—Com—Int	7-5-0	7-4-1
Third down efficiency	2-3	2-4

Second Quarter
49ERS
4/8/S12 15:00 Miller punted 44 yards to Fuller on his 44 and he returned 5 (Gervais).

BENGALS
1/10/C49 14:50 Johnson tried right guard and made five yards (Reese).
2/5/S46 Bengals time out. Anderson passed complete to Collinsworth for 18, **first down** (Lott).
1/10/S28 Cincinnati **penalty**, five yards, false start, on Lapham.
1/15/S33 Anderson's pass meant for Ross was ruled incomplete when it was trapped, not caught.
2/15/S33 San Francisco **penalty**; five yards, illegal contact, Thomas, **Bengals first down.**

1/10/S28   Alexander tried right tackle and made one yard (Harper).
2/9/S27   Anderson passed complete to Collinsworth for 19 yards, Wright tackled him and stripped the ball loose and Thomas recovered for San Francisco on the 49er eight.

49ERS
1/10/S8   12:22 Davis (J.), hit right guard and made one yard (Harris).
2/9/S9   Ring ran over right end for two yards (Browner).
3/7/S11   Montana rolled right and passed complete to Solomon for 20, **first down** (ran o.b.)
1/10/S31   Montana ran wide around right end from pass formation for eight yards (Browner).
2/2/S39   Cooper ran wide around right end for 14 yards, **first down** (Browner).
1/10/C47   Patton ran right tackle for four yards (Kemp).
2/6/C43   Montana's pass meant for Solomon was incomplete.
3/6/C43   Montana passed complete to Clark for 12 yards and a **first down** (Breeden).
1/10/C31   Patton drove up the middle for nine yards (Riley).
2/1/C22   Patton hit right tackle for three yards and a **first down** (Breeden).
1/10/C19   Clark, on an end-around left to right, lost two yards and after the play the Bengals were **penalized** ten yards for personal foul (on LeClair), 49ers **first down** on the 11.
1/10/C11   *Montana passed complete to Cooper on the three and Cooper ran into the end zone for an 11-yard touchdown and a first down.*
            Wersching, with Montana holding, converted.

            S.F. 14   CIN 0   DRIVE: 92 YDs, 12 P (8:07)

Wersching kicked off for San Francisco to Verser on the five and he returned minus one yard to the four (Wright). **Bengals penalty,** two yards, illegal chuck.

BENGALS
1/10/C2   6:42 Johnson hit center for four yards (Reese).
2/6/C6   Anderson passed complete to Ross over the right side for ten, **first down** (Reynolds).
1/10/C16   Anderson's pass meant for Curtis was just out of his reach, incomplete, at the 30.
2/10/C16   Anderson's pass meant for Ross was off his fingertips, incomplete.

3/10/C16 Anderson passed complete to Ross over the right side for nine yards (Leopold).
4/1/C25 McInally punted 47 yards to Hicks on his 28 and he returned six yards (Hargrove).

49ERS

1/10/S34 4:11 Montana passed complete to Clark for 17 yards, **first down** (Kemp) (13P-4R).
1/10/C49 Patton hit center for three yards (Whitley).
2/7/C46 Patton hit left guard for seven yards and a **first down** (Williams).
1/10/C39 Montana passed complete to Cooper over the right side for four yards (Breeden).
2/6/C35 1:57 Montana's pass meant for Young was broken up by Cameron.
3/6/C35 1:51 Montana passed complete to Clark for ten yards, **first down** (Riley).
1/10/C25 1:11 Patton ran wide around left end for three yards (Williams).
2/7/C22 1:06 Cooper found a hole at left guard for six yards (Browner).
3/1/C16 0:54 SF t.o. Montana sneaked over center for two, **first down** (Cameron).
1/10/C14 0:32 Montana passed complete to Solomon for nine (Breeden).
2/1/C5 0:29 Montana's pass for Clark was broken up by Cameron at the goal line.
3/1/C5 0:23 Montana's pass was high over the end zone, incomplete.
4/1/C5 0:18 **Wersching, with Montana holding, kicked a 22-yard field goal at 14:45.**

S.F. 17   CIN 0   DRIVE: 61 YDs, 13 P

Wersching kicked off for San Francisco to A. Griffin at the 15, he fumbled, the ball rolled backwards and McColl recovered at the four for San Francisco. 11 yards loose ball yardage.

49ERS

1/4/C4 0:05 49er **penalty,** illegal procedure, five yards.
1/9/C9 0:05 **Wersching, with Montana holding, kicked a 26-yard field goal at 14:58.**

S.F. 20   CIN 0   DRIVE: 0 YDs, 1 P

0:02 Wersching kicked off to Frazier on the Bengal 28 where he fell on the ball and time ran out.

[142]

HALFTIME SCORE: S.F. 20 CIN 0

	S.F.	CIN
First downs	15	7
Net yards rush	76	26
Net yards pass	132	73
Att—Com—Int	18-12-0	14-8-1
Third down efficiency	6-8	2-5

Third quarter: Wersching, with the south goal at his back, kicked off for San Francisco to Verser on the one and he returned 16 yards to his 17 (McColl).

BENGALS

1/10/C17 14:52 Alexander raced around right end for 13 yards and a **first down**; on the play, San Francisco was **penalized** five yards for face mask, another **Bengals first down** (Hicks).

1/10/C35 Johnson made three yards at right end (Harper).

2/7/C38 Anderson passed complete to Alexander in the right flat for three (Williamson).

3/4/C41 Anderson passed complete to Kreider for 19 yards (all pass), **first down** (Lott).

1/10/S40 Johnson broke through right guard for a quick five yards (Reese).

2/5/S35 Anderson handed off to Griffin who lateralled back to Anderson who passed complete to Curtis for 13 yards and a **first down** (Wright): Also, **SF penalty**, 11 yards, face mask which gave the Bengals another **first down.**

1/10/S11 Griffin hit center for four yards (Stuckey).

2/6/S7 Johnson ran left end for two yards (Reynolds).

3/4/S5 ***Anderson faded back to pass, then ran up the middle into the end zone for a five-yard touchdown and a first down.*** 49er **penalty**, 12 men on the field, assessed on kickoff.

Breech, with Kreider holding, converted.

S.F. 20   CIN 7   **DRIVE: 83 YDs 9 P (3:35)**

Breech, kicking from his 40, kicked off out of bounds, but no penalty was called for that because Leopold of San Francisco personal fouled and that 15-yard **penalty** prevailed. Breech, now kicking off from 49er 45, went through the end zone for a touchback.

49ERS
- 1/10/S20 11:13 Montana was sacked for a passing loss of nine yards (Browner).
- 2/19/S11 Montana's pass for Solomon was broken up by Breeden.
- 3/19/S11 Patton tried to circle right end and made four yards (Williams).
- 4/15/S15 Miller punted 47 yards to Fuller on his 38 and he returned 13 yards (Turner).

BENGALS
- 1/10/S49 9:35 Johnson drove over right guard for three yards (Board).
- 2/7/S46 Anderson's low pass in the left flat for Collinsworth was incomplete.
- 3/7/S46 Anderson ran around right end for no gain (Leopold chased him out of bounds).
- 4/7/S46 McInally punted 31 yards to Solomon who fair-caught it on his 15. SF refused motion.

49ERS
- 1/10/S15 8:34 Cooper tried left end and lost two yards to the 13 (LeClair).
- 2/12/S13 Ring tried to go inside right end and made one yard to the 14 (Edwards).
- 3/11/S14 Montana ran right and passed complete to Ring for three yards (R. Griffin).
- 4/8/S17 Miller punted 50 yards to Fuller on the Bengal 33 and he returned 17 yards (Turner).

BENGALS
- 1/10/50 6:53 Bengals Anderson ran right end for one yard (Harper); on the play, Cincinnati was **penalized** ten yards for holding, on Ross, back to the 41.
- 1/19/C41 Anderson passed complete to Ross for 15 yards (Wright). Now there's a 15-yard **penalty** on Cincinnati for personal foul.
- 2/19/C41 Anderson was sacked for a passing loss of four (Dean).
- 3/23/C37 Anderson passed complete to Collinsworth for 49 yards and a **first down** (Wright).
- 1/10/S14 Alexander made a yard at center (Reynolds).
- 2/9/S13 Anderson was sacked for minus two yards (Reynolds).
- 3/11/S15 Anderson passed complete to Ross for ten yards (Williamson).
- 4/1/S5 Johnson hit center for two, **first down** (Board).
- 1/3/S3 Johnson hit center for two (Dean).
- 2/1/S1 Johnson hit left guard for no gain (Harty).

3/1/S1   Anderson passed complete to Alexander for no gain (Bunz).
4/1/S1   Bengals took time out. Johnson tried center and was stopped for no gain (entire middle of the line).

49ERS
1/10/S1   1:17   Ring hit right end for three yards (Cameron).
2/7/S4   Ring hit right tackle and made four (Kemp). LeClair limped off.
3/3/S8   Time ran out on the quarter at this point.

END OF THE QUARTER: S.F. 20   CIN 7

	S.F.	CIN
First downs	15	15
Net yards rush	86	67
Net yards pass	126	176
Att—Com—Int	20-13-0	22-15-0
Third down efficiency	6-10	5-11

Fourth Quarter
49ERS
3/3/S8   15:00   Cooper on a draw at center made one (Browner).
4/2/S9   Miller punted 44 yards to Fuller on his 47 and he was dropped there (Cross).

BENGALS
1/10/C47   13:58   Johnson hit center for three (Stuckey).
2/7/50   Anderson passed complete up the middle to Collinsworth for 12, **first down** (Harper).
1/10/S38   Anderson passed complete up the middle to Ross for nine yards (Leopold).
2/1/S29   San Fransisco **penalty,** 14 yards, pass interference, on Lott, Bengals **first down.**
1/10/S15   Anderson's pass was incomplete, into the turf.
2/10/S15   Anderson passed complete to Ross for nine yards (Williamson).
3/1/S6   Alexander drove into center for two yards and a **first down** (Hicks).
1/4/S4   ***Anderson passed complete in the end zone to Ross for a four-yard touchdown and a first down.***
Breech, with Kreider holding, converted.

S.F. 20   CIN 14   **DRIVE: 53 YDs, 7 P (4:54)**

Breech kicked off for Cincinnati to Hicks on his four and he returned 23 yards (Razzano).

49ERS

1/10/S27 9:57 Montana's pass meant for Patton was broken up by Williams.

2/10/S27 San Fransisco **penalty,** five yards, false start, on Audick.

2/15/S22 Montana passed complete to Wilson (all pass) for 22 yards, **first down** (fell o.b.).

1/10/S44 Bengals **penalty,** five yards, pass interference, on Riley, 49ers **first down.**

1/10/S49 Patton broke over right guard for ten yards and a **first down** (Hicks).

1/10/C41 Patton hit right guard and picked up two yards (Browner).

2/8/C39 Patton drove over right tackle and made seven yards (Browner).

3/1/C32 Montana sneaked inside right tackle for four yards and a **first down** (Razzano).

1/10/C28 Cooper hit over left end for one yard (Riley).

2/9/C27 Patton drove over left tackle for three yards (Williams).

3/6/C24 Patton tried center and made one yard (Williams).

4/5/C23 ***Wersching, with Montana holding, kicked a 40-yard field goal at 9:35.***

        S.F. 23   CIN 14   **DRIVE: 50 YDs, 10 P**

Wersching kicked off to Verser on his 14 and he returned eight yards (Lawrence).

BENGALS

1/10/C22 5:14 Anderson's pass meant for Collinsworth was intercepted by Wright on the Bengals 47 and he returned it 25 yards to the 22 when he fumbled (Montoya) and Harper recovered.

49ERS

1/10/C22 4:57 Patton hit outside right tackle for four yards (Razzano).

2/6/C18 Cooper hit right guard for three yards (Cameron).

3/3/C15 J. Davis hit left guard down to the ten for four yards, **first down** (Hicks).

1/10/C11 Patton ran around right end for four yards (Breeden). Bengals, second time out.

2/6/C7 Patton tried to run around right end but was dropped for minus six yards (Razzano).

3/12/C13 Bengals t.o. (3). Montana bootlegged around left end for seven yards (Hicks).

4/5/C6   2:00 **Wersching, with Montana holding, kicked a 23-yard field goal at 13:03.**

S.F. 26   CIN 14   **DRIVE: 16 YDs, 7 P**

Wersching kicked off for San Fransisco to Verser on the 11 and he returned 15 yards (Lott).

BENGALS

1/10/C26 1:51 Anderson passed complete to Curtis for 21, **first down** (Williamson).

1/10/C47 1:26 Anderson passed to Ross for 16 yards, **first down** (Williamson).

1/10/S37 1:00 Anderson passed to Ross for eight yards (Harper).

2/2/S29 0:40 Anderson passed to Collinsworth for nine yards and a **first down** (Leopold).

1/10/S20 0:25 Anderson passed to Kreider for 17, **first down** (Leopold).

1/3/S3 0:20 **Anderson passed complete to Ross in the end zone, 3-yard touchdown, first down.**

Breech, with Kreider holding, converted.

S.F. 26   CIN 21   **DRIVE: 89 YDs, 6 P (14:44)**

Breech's onside kickoff was recovered by Clark of San Francisco on the San Francisco 48.

49ERS

1/10/S48

0:14 Montana lost four yards on a quarterback fall-down play and time ran out.

FINAL SCORE OF SUPER BOWL XVI
SAN FRANSISCO 26   CINCINNATI 21

	S.F.	CIN
First downs	20	24
Net yards rush	127	72
Net yards pass	148	284
Att—Com—Int	22-14-0	34-25-2
Third down efficiency	8-15	6-12

GAME SUMMARY

Visitor: San Francisco 49ers   **vs.**   **Home:** Cincinnati Bengals
Date: 24 January 1982   **At:** Pontiac Silverdome
Day of Week: Sunday   **Starting Time:** 4:20 P.M.
Weather: Domed stadium
Temperature: 72°F   **Wind and Direction:** NESW 1 mph
ATTENDANCE:
Tickets Distributed: **Actual:** 81,270   **Time:** 3:21

SCORING BY QUARTER

	1	2	3	4	OT	TOTAL
San Francisco 49ers	7	13	0	6		26
Cincinnati Bengals	0	0	7	14		21

SCORING BY PLAY AND DRIVE

Team	Per.	Elapsed Time	Scoring Play	Score Vis.	Home
SF	1	9:08	Montana 1 run (Wersching kick) (11–68)	7	0
SF	2	8:07	Cooper 11 pass from Montana (Wersching kick) (12–92)	14	0
SF	2	14:45	FG Wersching (13–61)	17	0
SF	2	14:58	FG Wersching 26 (1–0)	20	0
CIN	3	3:35	Anderson 5 run (Breech kick) (9–83)	20	7
CIN	4	4:54	Ross 4 pass from Anderson (Breech kick) (7–53)	20	14
SF	4	9:35	FG Wersching 40 (10–50)	23	14
SF	4	13:03	FG Wersching 23 (7–16)	26	14
CIN	4	14:44	Ross 3 pass from Anderson (Breech kick) (6–74)	26	21

FINAL TEAM STATISTICS

	49ERS	BENGALS
Total first downs	20	24
By rushing	9	7
By passing	9	13
By penalty	2	4
Third down efficiency	8/15–53.0%	6/12–50.0%
Total net yards	275	356
Total offensive plays*	63	63
Average gain per offensive play	4.4	5.7
Net yards rushing	127	72
Total rushing plays	40	24
Average gain per rushing play	3.2	3.0
Net yards passing	148	284
Times thrown/yds. lost att. to pass	1/9	5/16
Gross yards passing	157	300
Pass atts./completions/had intercepted	22/14/0	34/25/2
Avg. gain per pass play*	6.4	7.3
Punts—number/average	4/46.3	3/43.7
Had blocked	0	0
Total return yardage	98	87
Number/yards punt returns	1/6	4/35
Number/yards kickoff returns	3/40	7/52
Number/yards interception returns	2/52	0/0
Penalties—number/yards	8/65	8/57
Fumbles—number/lost	2/1	2/2
Touchdowns	2	3
Rushing	1	1
Passing	1	2
Returns	0	0
Extra points made/attempts	2/2	3/3
Field goals made/attempts	4/4	0/0
Time of possession	32:13	27:47

*Includes times thrown passing

INDIVIDUAL TEAM STATISTICS

Cincinnati Bengals

Rushing	Att	Yds	Avg	LG	TD
Johnson	14	36	2.6	5	0
Alexander	5	17	3.4	13	0
Anderson	4	15	3.8	6	1
Griffin, A.	1	4	4.0	4	0
TOTAL	24	72	3.0	13	1

Passing	Att	Cp	Yds	TD	LG	Int	Tk/Yds
Anderson	34	25	300	2	49	2	5/16
TOTAL	34	25	300	2	49	2	5/16

Receiving	No	Yds	LG	TD
Curtis	3	42	21	0
Ross	11	104	16	2
Johnson	2	8	5	0
Collinsworth	5	107	49	0
Alexander	2	3	3	0
Kreider	2	36	19	0
TOTAL	25	300	49	2

Interceptions	No	Yds	Avg	LG	TD
TOTAL	0	0	0.0	0	0

Punting	No	Yds	Avg	TB	In 20	LP
McInally	3	131	43.7	0	2	53
TOTAL	3	131	43.7	0	2	53

Punt Returns	No	FC	Yds	Avg	LG	TD
Fuller	4	0	35		17	0
TOTAL	4	0	35		17	0

Kickoff Rets	No	Yds	Avg	LG	TD
Verser	5	52		16	0
Griffin, A.	1	0		0	0
Frazier	1	0		0	0
TOTAL	7	52		16	0

Fumbles	No	Own Rec	Own Yds	Own TD	Opp Rec	Opp Yds	Opp TD	OB
Simmons	0	0	0	0	1	0	0	0
Collinsworth	1	0	0	0	0	0	0	0
Griffin, A.	1	0	0	0	0	0	0	0
TOTAL	2	0	0	0	1	0	0	0

San Francisco 49ers

Rushing	Att	Yds	Avg	LG	TD
Cooper	9	34	3.8	14	0
Ring	5	17	3.4	7	0
Montana	6	18	3.0	7	1
Patton	17	55	3.2	10	0
Davis, J.	2	5	2.5	4	0
Clark	1	−2	−2.0	−2	0
TOTAL	40	127	3.2	14	1

Passing	Att	Cp	Yds	TD	LG	Int	Tk/Yds
Montana	22	14	157	1	22	0	1/9
TOTAL	22	14	157	1	22	0	1/9

Receiving	No	Yds	LG	TD
Patton	1	6	6	0
Clark	4	45	17	0
Solomon	4	52	20	0
Young	1	14	14	0
Cooper	2	15	11	1
Ring	1	3	3	0
Wilson	1	22	22	0
TOTAL	14	157	22	1

Interceptions	No	Yds	Avg	LG	TD
Hicks	1	27		27	0
TOTAL	1	27		27	0

Punting	No	Yds	Avg	TB	In 20	LP
Miller	4	185	46.3	0	0	50
TOTAL	4	185	46.3	0	0	50

Punt Returns	No	FC	Yds	Avg	LG	TD
Hicks	1	0	6		6	0
Solomon	0	1	0		0	0
TOTAL	1	1	6		6	0

Kickoff Rets	No	Yds	Avg	LG	TD
Lawrence	1	17		17	0
Hicks	1	23		23	0
Clark	1	0		0	0
TOTAL	3	40		23	0

Fumbles	No	Own Rec	Yds	TD	Opp Rec	Yds	TD	OB
Lawrence	1	0	0	0	0	0	0	0
Thomas	0	0	0	0	1	0	0	0
McCall	0	0	0	0	1	0	0	0
Wright	1	0	0	0	0	0	0	0
Harper	0	1	0	0	0	0	0	0
TOTAL	2	1	0	0	2	0	0	0

FIRST DOWN PLAYS—YARDS GAINED

San Francisco 49ers

All Plays

Qtr.	No.	Total Gain	Avg. Gain	First Downs	Turnovers
1	6	14	2.3	0	0
2	11	65	5.9	1	0
3	2	1	0.5	0	0
4	7	25	3.6	0	0
TOTAL	26	105	4.0	1	0

Rushing Plays

Qtr.	No.	Total Gain	Avg. Gain	First Downs	Turnovers
1	3	8	2.7	0	0
2	7	26	3.7	0	0
3	2	1	0.5	0	0
4	5	21	4.2	0	0
TOTAL	17	56	3.3	0	0

Passing Plays

Qtr.	No.	Total Gain	Avg. Gain	First Downs	Turnovers
1	3	6	2.0	0	0
2	4	39	9.8	1	0
3	0	0	0.0	0	0
4	2	5	2.5	1	0
TOTAL	7	50	7.1	1	0

Cincinnati Bengals

All Plays

Qtr.	No.	Total Gain	Avg. Gain	First Downs	Turnovers
1	6	25	4.2	1	0
2	4	9	2.3	0	0
3	8	32	4.0	0	0
4	10	77	7.7	6	1
TOTAL	28	143	5.1	7	1

Rushing Plays

Qtr.	No.	Total Gain	Avg. Gain	First Downs	Turnovers
1	2	3	1.5	0	0
2	3	9	3.0	0	0
3	8	32	4.0	0	0
4	1	3	3.0	0	0
TOTAL	14	47	3.4	0	0

Qtr.	No.	Passing Plays Total Gain	Avg. Gain	First Downs	Turn overs
1	4	22	5.5	1	0
2	1	0	0.0	0	0
3	0	0	0.0	0	0
4	9	74	8.2	6	1
TOTAL	14	96	6.9	7	

THIRD DOWN CONVERSION SUMMARY

San Francisco 49ers

No.	Yard Line	To Go	Player/Type of Play*	Result	FD	Comments
1	C47	1	Young/P	14	x	
2	C15	3	Solomon/P	14	x	
3	S8	12	Patton/R	4		
4	S11	7	Solomon/P	20	x	
5	C43	6	Clark/P	12	x	
6	C35	6	Clark/P	10	x	
7	C16	1	Montana/R	2	x	
8	C5	1	Out of bounds/P	Inc		
9	S11	9	Patton/R	4		
10	S14	11	Ring/P	3		
11	S8	3	Cooper/R	1		
12	C32	1	Montana/R	4	x	
13	C24	6	Patton/R	1		
14	C15	3	Davis/R	4	x	
15	C13	12	Montana/R	7		

*Type of Play: R-Rush; P-Pass

Cincinnati Bengals

No.	Yard Line	To Go	Player/Type of Play*	Result	FD	Comments
1	S10	10	Curtis/P	Int		Hicks 27 yd return
2	C27	2	Anderson/R	3	x	
3	C39	1	Johnson/R	2	x	
4	C41	9	Sack	4		Torner
5	C16	10	Ross/P	9		
6	C41	4	Kreider/P	19	x	
7	S5	4	Anderson/R	6	x	TD
8	S46	7	Anderson/R	0	x	sack
9	C37	23	Collinsworth/P	49	x	
10	S15	11	Ross/P	10		
11	S1	1	Alexander/P	0		
12	S6	1	Alexander/R	2	x	

Type of Play: R-Rush; P-Pass

Records set in Super Bowl XVI

RECORDS SET

Most Passes Completed, Game—25, Ken Anderson, Cincinnati (old record: 18, Fran Tarkenton VIII, Ron Jaworski XV)

Highest Completion Percentage, Game (minimum: 20 attempts)—73.5, 25-of-34, Ken Anderson, Cincinnati (old record: 69.6, Bart Starr I)

Most Pass Receptions, Game—11, Dan Ross, Cincinnati (old record: 8, George Sauer, III)

Largest Halftime Lead, Team—20-0, San Francisco vs. Cincinnati (old record: 17-0, Miami vs. Minnesota VIII)

Longest Scoring Drive, Team—92 yards, San Francisco vs. Cincinnati (old record: 89 yards, Dallas vs. Pittsburgh XIII)

Most First Downs, Game, Team—24, Cincinnati vs. San Francisco (old record: 23, Dallas vs. Miami VI)

Most First Downs, Game, Both Teams—44, Cincinnati (24) vs San Francisco (20) (old record: 41, Oakland and Minnesota XI)

Most First Downs by Penalty, Game Both Teams—6, Cincinnati (4) vs. San Francisco (2) (old record: 5, accomplished twice)

Most Passes Completed, Game, Team—25, Cincinnati vs. San Francisco (old record: 24, Minnesota vs. Oakland XI)

Most Passes Completed, Game, Both Teams—39, Cincinnati (25) vs. San Francisco (14) (old record: 36, Minnesota and Oakland XI)

Highest Completion Percentage, Game, Team—73.5, 25-of-34, Cincinnati vs. San Francisco (old record: 67.9, Dallas vs. Denver XII)

Chapter 12

The 1981 Season Game by Game

The following game statistics reproduce official National Football League charts, issued after each game at the site. Where there are inconsistencies or blanks, they exist that way on the original sheets, which were compiled by different sets of statisticians in different press boxes.

This material, and the material presented in the previous chapter, is copyrighted and is used with permission.

GAME SUMMARY

Visitor: San Francisco 49ers   **vs.**   **Home:** Detroit Lions
Date: 6 September 1981   **At:** Pontiac Silverdome
Day of Week: Sunday   **Starting Time:** 1:03 P.M.
Weather: Dome controlled
Temperature: 70°F   **Wind and Direction:** N-E-S-W 1 mph
ATTENDANCE:
Tickets Distributed: 63,710   **Actual:** 62,123   **Time:** 3:03

SCORING BY QUARTER

	1	2	3	4	OT	TOTAL
San Francisco 49ers	0	3	0	14		17
Detroit Lions	0	10	0	14		24

SCORING BY PLAY AND DRIVE

Team	Per.	Elapsed Time	Scoring Play	Vis.	Home
SF	2	10:32	FG Wersching, 25 (8–37)	3	0
DET	2	14:32	Sims 39 pass from Danielson (Murray kick) (9–85)	3	7
DET	2	15:00	FG Murray 29 (3–14)	3	10
SF	4	0:06	Patton 1 run (Wersching kick) (16–55)	10	10
DET	4	4:29	King 17 pass from Danielson (Murray kick) (9–64)	10	17
SF	4	7:30	Solomon 21 pass from Montana (Wersching kick) (7–74)	17	17
DET	4	14:42	Sims 1 run (Murray kick) (8–50)	17	24

FINAL TEAM STATISTICS

	49ERS	LIONS
Total first downs	19	21
By rushing	6	9
By passing	10	9
By penalty	3	3
Third down efficiency	6/14–43%	6/11–55%
Total net yards	297	295
Total offensive plays*	65	61
Average gain per offensive play	4.6	4.8
Net yards rushing	121	127
Total rushing plays	33	30
Average gain per rushing play	3.7	4.2
Net yards passing	176	168
Times thrown/yds. lost att. to pass	4/19	4/28
Gross yards passing	195	196
Pass atts./completions/had intercepted	28/18/1	27/16/1
Avg. gain per pass play*	5.5	5.4
Punts—number/average	3/33.7	4/46.3
Had blocked	0	0
Total return yardage	105	47
Number/yards punt returns	4/62	1/11
Number/yards kickoff returns	3/43	3/36
Number/yards interception returns	1/0	1/0
Penalties—number/yards	8/54	7/65
Fumbles—number/lost	2/2	1/1
Touchdowns	2	3
Rushing	1	1
Passing	1	2
Returns	0	0
Extra points made/attempts	2/2	3/3
Field goals made/attempts	1/2	1/2
Time of possession	31:56	28:04

*Includes times thrown passing

DETROIT LIONS

Rushing	Att	Yds	Avg	LG	TD
Sims	21	59	2.8	14	1
Bussey	4	23	5.8	16	0
L. Thompson	1	17	17.0	17	0
King	2	10	5.0	5	0
V. Thompson	1	12	12.0	12	0
Danielson	1	6	6.0	6	0
TOTAL	30	127	4.2	17	1

Passing	Att	Cp	Yds	TD	LG	Int	Tk/Yds
Danielson	27	16	196	2	39	1	4/28
TOTAL	27	16	196	2	39	1	4/28

Receiving	No	Yds	LG	TD
Sims	5	66	39	1
L. Thompson	3	63	28	0
King	3	24	17	1
Scott	2	23	16	0
Norris	2	15	8	0
Kane	1	5	5	0
TOTAL	16	196	39	2

Interceptions	No	Yds	Avg	LG	TD
Allen	1	0	0	0	0
TOTAL	1	0	0	0	0

Punting	No	Yds	Avg	TB	In 20	LP
Skladany	4	185	46.3	0	1	50
TOTAL	4	185	46.3	0	1	50

Punt Returns	No	FC	Yds	Avg	LG	TD
Martin	1	0	11		11	0
TOTAL	1	0	11		11	0

Kickoff Rets	No	Yds	Avg	LG	TD
Hall	2	17		17	0
King	2	19		12	0
TOTAL	4	36		17	0

Fumbles	No	Own Rec	Yds	TD	Opp Rec	Yds	TD	OB
English	0	0	0	0	1	0	0	0
Sims	1	0	0	0	0	0	0	0
Gay	0	0	0	0	1	0	0	0
TOTAL	1	0	0	0	2	0	0	0

SAN FRANCISCO 49ERS

Rushing	Att	Yds	Avg	LG	TD
Patton	15	72	4.8	22	1
Easley	7	23	3.3	6	0
Cooper	9	22	2.4	9	0
Montana	2	4	2.0	10	0
TOTAL	33	121	4.0	22	1

Passing	Att	Cp	Yds	Td	Lg	Int	Tk/Yds
Montana	28	18	195	1	23	1	4/19
TOTAL	28	18	195	1	23	1	4/19

Receiving	No	Yds	LG	TD
Solomon	8	94	21	1
Clark	5	57	17	0
Cooper	3	11	5	0
Young	2	33	23	0
TOTAL	18	195	23	1

Interceptions	No	Yds	Avg	LG	TD
Reynolds	1	0	0	0	0
TOTAL	1	0	0	0	0

Punting	No	Yds	Avg	TB	In 20	LP
Miller	3	101	33.7	1	0	46
TOTAL	3	101	33.7	1	0	46

Punt Returns	No	FC	Yds	Avg	LG	TD
Hicks	2	0	46	23	39	0
Solomon	2	0	16	8	8	0
TOTAL	4	0	62	15.5	39	0

Kickoff Rets	No	Yds	Avg	LG	TD
Jones	3	43		22	0
Patton	1	0		0	0
TOTAL	4	43		22	0

Fumbles	No	Own Rec	Own Yds	Own TD	Opp Rec	Opp Yds	Opp TD	OB
Cooper	1	0	0	0	0	0	0	0
Harper	0	0	0	0	1	0	0	0
Jones, A.	1	0	0	0	0	0	0	0
TOTAL	2	0	0	0	1	0	0	0

GAME SUMMARY

Visitor: Chicago Bears   **vs.**   **Home:** San Francisco 49ers
Date: 13 September 1981   **At:** Candlestick Park, SF
Day of Week: Sunday   **Starting Time:** 1:01 P.M.
Weather: Mostly sunny with intermittent clouds
Temperature: 68°F   **Wind and Direction:** N-NW 30 mph

ATTENDANCE:
Tickets Distributed: 53,706   **Actual:** 49,520   **Time:** 3:00

SCORING BY QUARTER

	1	2	3	4	OT	TOTAL
Chicago Bears	0	10	7	0		17
San Francisco 49ers	7	7	7	7		28

SCORING BY PLAY AND DRIVE

Team	Per.	Elapsed Time	Scoring Play	Vis.	Home
SF	1	9:37	Montanta 31 pass to Patton (Bahr kick)—70 yds, 6P	0	7
SF	2	3:08	Montanta 46 pass to Solomon (Bahr kick)—46 yds, 1P	0	14
CHI	2	8:33	Payton 2 run (Thomas kick)—4 yds, 2P	7	14
CHI	2	14:28	Thomas FG 37—30 yds, 7P	10	14
CHI	3	3:24	Evans 12 pass to Earl (Thomas kick)—68 yds, 10P	17	14
SF	3	9:19	Montana 5 pass to Young (Bahr kick)—33 yds, 2P	17	21
SF	4	13:35	Patton 12 run (Bahr kick)—50 yds, 8P	17	28

FINAL TEAM STATISTICS

	BEARS	49ERS
Total first downs	18	20
By rushing	7	5
By passing	11	13
By penalty	0	2
Third down efficiency	5/12–41.7%	5/14–35.7%
Total net yards	339	412
Total offensive plays*	70	64
Average gain per offensive play	4.8	6.4
Net yards rushing	123	125
Total rushing plays	36	32
Average gain per rushing play	3.4	3.9
Net yards passing	216	287
Times thrown/yds. lost att. to pass	1/0	0/0
Gross yards passing	216	287
Pass atts./completions/had intercepted	33/19/1	32/20/0
Avg. gain per pass play*	6.4	9.0
Punts—number/average	6/41.5	5/38.0
Had blocked	0	0
Total return yardage	110	110
Number/yards punt returns	2/24	5/47
Number/yards kickoff returns	4/82	4/55
Number/yards interception returns	0/0	1/8
Penalties—number/yards	4/16	3/25
Fumbles—number/lost	2/2	2/2
Touchdowns	2	4
Rushing	1	1
Passing	1	3
Returns	0	0
Extra points made/attempts	2/2	4/4
Field goals made/attempts	1/2	0/2
Time of possession	25:16	34:44

*Includes times thrown passing

INDIVIDUAL TEAM STATISTICS

Chicago Bears

Rushing	Att	Yds	Avg	LG	TD
Payton	27	97	3.6	12	1
Suhey	6	25	4.2	15	0
Evans	2	7	3.5	5	0
Neal	1	−6	−6.0	−6	0
TOTAL	36	123	3.4	15	1

Passing	Att	Cp	Yds	TD	LG	Int	Tk/Yds
Evans	33	19	216	1	26	1	1/0
TOTAL	33	19	216	1	26	1	1/0

Receiving	No	Yds	LG	TD
Watts	5	74	17	0
Earl	4	48	24	1
Williams	4	25	12	0
Payton	3	11	5	0
Baschnagel	2	41	26	0
Margerum	1	17	17	0
TOTAL	19	216	26	1

Interceptions	No	Yds	Avg	LG	TD
TOTAL	0	0	0.0	0	0

Punting	No	Yds	Avg	TB	In 20	LP
Parsons	6	249	41.5	1	0	47
TOTAL	6	249	41.5	1	0	47

Punt Returns	No	FF	Yds	Avg	LG	TD
Fisher, J.	2	1	24	12.0	13	0
TOTAL	2	1	24	12.0	13	0

Kickoff Rets	No	Yds	Avg	LG	TD
Williams	3	59	19.7	29	0
Baschnagel	1	23	23.0	23	0
TOTAL	4	82	20.5	29	0

Fumbles	No	Own Rec	Own Yds	Own TD	Opp Rec	Opp Yds	Opp TD	OB
Payton	2	0	0	0	0	0	0	0
Plank	0	0	0	0	1	0	0	0
Hartenstine	0	0	0	0	1	4	0	0
TOTAL	2	0	0	0	2	4	0	0

San Francisco 49ers

Rushing	Att	Yds	Avg	LG	TD
Patton	14	67	4.8	13	1
Cooper	14	56	4.0	23	0
Easley	3	5	1.7	6	0
Solomon	1	−3	−3.0	−3	0
TOTAL	32	125	3.9	23	1

Passing	Att	Cp	Yds	TD	LG	Int	Tk/Yds
Montana	32	20	287	3	46	0	0/0
TOTAL	32	20	287	3	46	0	0/0

Receiving	No	Yds	LG	TD
Clark	6	81	23	0
Solomon	5	113	46	1
Cooper	4	28	20	0
Patton	2	34	31	1
Young	2	19	14	1
Elliott	1	12	12	0
TOTAL	20	287	46	3

Interceptions	No	Yds	Avg	LG	TD
Hicks	1	8	8.0	8	0
TOTAL	1	8	8.0	8	0

Punting	No	Yds	Avg	TB	In 20	LP
Miller	5	190	38.0	0	1	52
TOTAL	5	190	38.0	0	1	52

Punt Returns	No	FC	Yds	Avg	LG	TD
Solomon	4	0	40	10.0	19	0
Hicks	1	0	7	7.0	7	0
TOTAL	5	0	47	9.4	19	0

Kickoff Rets	No	Yds	Avg	LG	TD
Lott	3	55	18.3	20	0
Davis	1	0	0.0	0	0
TOTAL	4	55	13.8	20	0

Fumbles	No	Own Rec	Own Yds	Own TD	Opp Rec	Opp Yds	Opp TD	OB
Elliott	1	0	0	0	0	0	0	0
Quillan	1	0	0	0	0	0	0	0
Bunz	0	0	0	0	1	0	0	0
Puki	0	0	0	0	1	0	0	0
TOTAL	2	0	0	0	2	0	0	0

GAME SUMMARY

Visitor: San Francisco 49ers   **vs.**   **Home:** Atlanta Falcons
Date: 20 September 1981   **At:** Atlanta, Ga.
Day of Week: Sunday   **Starting Time:** 1:01 P.M.
Weather: Clear
Temperature: 70°F   **Wind and Direction:** NW 9 mph

ATTENDANCE:
Tickets Distributed: 59,719   **Actual:** 56,653   **Time:** 2:31

SCORING BY QUARTER

	1	2	3	4	OT	TOTAL
San Francisco 49ers	0	10	0	7		17
Atlanta Falcons	17	7	10	0		34

SCORING BY PLAY AND DRIVE

Team	Per.	Elapsed Time	Scoring Play	Vis.	Home
ATL	1	3:39	Jackson 29 pass from Bartkowski (Luckhurst kick)	0	7
ATL	1	9:46	FG Luckhurst 47	0	10
ATL	1	11:03	Cain 18 pass from Bartkowski (Luckhurst kick)	0	17
SF	2	1:28	Young 11 pass from Montana (Bahr kick)	7	17
SF	2	6:05	FG Bahr 47	10	0
ATL	2	10:03	Jenkins 15 pass from Bartkowski (Luckhurst kick)	10	24
ATL	3	5:21	Pridemore 101 interception return (Luckhurst kick)	10	31
ATL	3	10:56	FG Luckhurst 18	10	34
SF	4	8:50	Solomon 12 pass from Montana (Bahr kick)	17	34

FINAL TEAM STATISTICS

	49ERS	FALCONS
Total first downs	23	18
By rushing	6	6
By passing	16	10
By penalty	1	2
Third down efficiency	5/11–45%	6/12–50%
Total net yards	386	363
Total offensive plays*	65	59
Average gain per offensive play	5.9	6.2
Net yards rushing	113	163
Total rushing plays	30	34
Average gain per rushing play	3.8	4.8
Net yards passing	273	200
Times thrown/yds. lost att. to pass	1/1	2/22
Gross yards passing	274	222
Pass atts./completions/had intercepted	34/24/2	23/14/0
Avg. gain per pass play*	7.8	8.0
Punts—number/average	34/53.3	3/36.7
Had blocked	0	0
Total return yardage	118	199
Number/yards punt returns	2/17	2/18
Number/yards kickoff returns	5/101	2/55
Number/yards interception returns	0/0	2/126
Penalties—number/yards	3/25	4/50
Fumbles—number/lost	1/1	2/0
Touchdowns	2	4
Rushing	0	0
Passing	2	3
Returns	0	1
Extra points made/attempts	2/2	4/4
Field goals made/attempts	1/2	2/3
Time of possession	32:08	27:52

*Includes times thrown passing

INDIVIDUAL TEAM STATISTICS

San Francisco 49ers

Rushing	Att	Yds	Avg	LG	TD
Patton	12	30	2.5	9	0
Cooper	9	40	4.4	7	0
Solomon	1	8	8.0	8	0
Elliott	4	17	4.3	9	0
Easley	4	18	4.5	6	0
TOTAL	30	113	3.8	9	0

Passing	Att	Cp	Yds	TD	LG	Int	Tk/Yds
Montana	34	24	274	2	27	2	1/1
TOTAL	34	24	274	2	27	2	1/1

Receiving	No	Yds	LG	TD
Clark	9	77	21	0
Cooper	3	29	11	0
Young	3	55	27	1
Solomon	3	36	23	1
Patton	2	16	13	0
Hofer	1	22	22	0
Peets	1	5	5	0
Wilson	2	34	21	0
TOTAL	24	274	27	2

Interceptions	No	Yds	Avg	LG	TD
TOTAL	0	0	0.0	0	0

Punting	No	Yds	Avg	TB	In 20	LP
Miller	3	160	53.3	1	1	57
TOTAL	3	160	53.3	1	1	57

Punt Returns	No	FC	Yds	Avg	LG	TD
Solomon	2	0	9		8	0
Hicks	0	1	0		0	0
TOTAL	2	1	9		8	0

Kickoff Rets	No	Yds	Avg	LG	TD
Lott	3	56		20	0
Ring	1	23		23	0
Wilson	1	22		22	0
TOTAL	5	101		23	0

Fumbles	No	Own Rec	Own Yds	Own TD	Opp Rec	Opp Yds	Opp TD	OB
Lott	1	0	0	0	0	0	0	0
TOTAL	1	0	0	0	0	0	0	0

Atlanta Falcons

Rushing	Att	Yds	Avg	LG	TD
Andrews	12	85	7.1	29	0
Cain	12	48	4.0	21	0
Robinson	6	19	3.2	5	0
Mayberry	3	12	4.0	6	0
Jones	1	−1	−1.0	−1	0
TOTAL	34	163	4.8	29	0

Passing	Att	Cp	Yds	TD	LG	Int	Tk/Yds
Bartkowski	22	13	208	3	67	0	2/22
Jones	1	1	14	0	14	0	0/0
TOTAL	23	14	222	3	67	0	2/22

Receiving	No	Yds	LG	TD
Andrews	4	37	14	0
Jackson	2	42	29	1
Cain	3	28	18	1
Miller	2	22	14	0
Francis	1	11	11	0
Jenkins	2	82	67	1
TOTAL	14	222	67	3

Interceptions	No	Yds	Avg	LG	TD
Williams	1	25		25	0
Pridemore	1	101		101	1
TOTAL	2	126		101	1

Punting	No	Yds	Avg	TB	In 20	LP
James	3	110	36.7	0	0	39
TOTAL	3	110	36.7	0	0	39

Punt Returns	No	FC	Yds	Avg	LG	TD
Smith, R.	1	0	9		9	0
Woerner	1	0	9		9	0
TOTAL	2	0	18		9	0

Kickoff Rets	No	Yds	Avg	LG	TD
Smith, R.	2	55		28	0
TOTAL	2	55		28	0

Fumbles	No	Own Rec	Yds	TD	Opp Rec	Yds	TD	OB
Andrews	1	0	0	0	0	0	0	0
Cain	1	1	0	0	0	0	0	0
Kenn	0	1	0	0	0	0	0	0
Strong	0	0	0	0	1	0	0	0
TOTAL	2	2	0	0	1	0	0	0

GAME SUMMARY

Visitor: New Orleans Saints **vs.** **Home:** San Francisco 49ers
Date: 27 September 1981 **At:** Candlestick Park, SF
Day of Week: Sunday **Starting Time:** 1:04 P.M.
Weather: Partly cloudy/rain 30%
Temperature: 68°F **Wind and Direction:** SW variable to 10 mph

ATTENDANCE:
Tickets Distributed: 49,860 **Actual:** 44,433 **Time:** 3:10

SCORING BY QUARTER

	1	2	3	4	OT	TOTAL
New Orleans Saints	7	0	0	7		14
San Francisco 49ers	0	7	7	7		21

SCORING BY PLAY AND DRIVE

Team	Per.	Elapsed Time	Scoring Play	Score Vis.	Home
NO	1	13:23	Groth 24 pass from D. Wilson (Ricardo kick)—80 yds, 7 plays	7	0
SF	2	5:08	Davis 6 run (Bahr kick)—69 yards, 15 plays	7	7
SF	3	3:12	Solomon 60 pass from Montana (Bahr kick)—62 yds, 2 plays	7	14
SF	4	3:28	Lott 26 interception return (Bahr kick)	7	21
NO	4	13:51	W. Wilson 9 pass from Manning (Ricardo kick)—80 yds, 14 plays	14	21

FINAL TEAM STATISTICS

	SAINTS	49ERS
Total first downs	18	15
By rushing	7	8
By passing	9	6
By penalty	2	1
Third down efficiency	6/18–33.3%	6/15–40.0%
Total net yards	413	314
Total offensive plays*	75	62
Average gain per offensive play	5.5	5.1
Net yards rushing	163	146
Total rushing plays	37	39
Average gain per rushing play	4.4	3.7
Net yards passing	250	168
Times thrown/yds. lost att. to pass	0/0	1/7
Gross yards passing	250	175
Pass atts./completions/had intercepted	38/21/2	22/16/1
Avg. gain per pass play*	6.6	7.3
Punts—number/average	6/40.2	9/45.1
Had blocked	0	0
Total return yardage	192	102
Number/yards punt returns	6/91	4/24
Number/yards kickoff returns	4/70	2/26
Number/yards interception returns	1/31	2/52
Penalties—number/yards	11/106	8/79
Fumbles—number/lost	3/2	1/1
Touchdowns	2	3
Rushing	0	1
Passing	2	1
Returns	0	1
Extra points made/attempts	2/2	3/3
Field goals made/attempts	0/0	0/0
Time of possession	30:44	29:16

*Includes times thrown passing

INDIVIDUAL TEAM STATISTICS

San Francisco 49ers

Rushing	Att	Yds	Avg	LG	TD
Davis	11	48	4.4	14	1
Patton	14	42	3.0	6	0
Hofer	4	19	4.8	7	0
Montana	3	17	5.7	14	0
Cooper	5	10	2.0	4	0
Solomon	1	5	5.0	5	0
Easley	1	5	5.0	5	0
TOTAL	39	146	3.7	14	1

Passing	Att	Cp	Yds	TD	LG	Int	Tk/Yds
Montana	22	16	175	1	60	1	1/7
TOTAL	22	16	175	1	60	1	1/7

Receiving	No	Yds	LG	TD
Young	3	41	25	0
Clark	3	30	14	0
Cooper	3	6	4	0
Solomon	2	80	60	1
Patton	2	8	5	0
Hofer	2	7	5	0
Lawrence	1	3	3	0
TOTAL	16	175	60	1

Interceptions	No	Yds	Avg	LG	TD
Wright	1	26	26.0	26	0
Lott	1	26	26.0	26	1
TOTAL	2	52	26.0	26	1

Punting	No	Yds	Avg	TB	In 20	LP
Miller	9	406	45.1	2	0	59
TOTAL	9	406	45.1	2	0	59

Punt Returns	No	FC	Yds	Avg	LG	TD
Solomon	3	2	14	4.7	9	0
Hicks	1	0	10	10.0	10	0
TOTAL	4	2	24	6.0	10	0

Kickoff Rets	No	Yds	Avg	LG	TD
Lawrence	1	26	26.0	26	0
Lott	1	0	0.0	0	0
TOTAL	2	26	13.0	26	0

Fumbles	No	Own Rec	Own Yds	Own TD	Opp Rec	Opp Yds	Opp TD	OB
Montana	1	0	0	0	0	0	0	0
Wright	0	0	0	0	1	0	0	0
Bunz	0	0	0	0	1	0	0	0
TOTAL	1	0	0	0	2	0	0	0

New Orleans Saints

Rushing	Att	Yds	Avg	LG	TD
Rogers, G.	25	115	4.6	13	0
Wilson, W.	5	27	5.4	12	0
Tyler	2	13	6.5	12	0
Wilson, D.	1	9	9.0	9	0
Holmes	3	8	2.7	4	0
Myers	1	−9	−9.0	0	0
TOTAL	37	163	4.4	13	0

Passing	Att	Cp	Yds	TD	LG	Int	Tk/Yds
Wilson, D.	22	11	180	1	39	1	0/0
Manning	16	10	70	1	11	1	0/0
TOTAL	38	21	250	2	39	2	0/0

Receiving	No	Yds	LG	TD
Chandler	4	72	39	0
Tyler	4	30	9	0
Holmes	3	11	10	1
Groth	2	56	32	1
Wilson, W.	2	27	18	1
Williams	2	17	11	0
Rogers, G.	2	16	9	0
Caster	1	13	13	0
Hardy	1	8	8	0
TOTAL	21	250	39	2

Interceptions	No	Yds	Avg	LG	TD
Waymer	1	31	31.0	31	0
TOTAL	1	31	31.0	31	0

Punting	No	Yds	Avg	TB	In 20	LP
Erxleben	6	241	40.2	0	1	47
TOTAL	6	241	40.2	0	1	47

Punt Returns	No	FC	Yds	Avg	LG	TD
Groth	6	0	91	15.2	36	0
Merkens	0	1	0	0.0	0	0
TOTAL	6	1	91	15.2	36	0

Kickoff Rets	No	Yds	Avg	LG	TD
Wilson, W.	1	21	21.0	21	0
Groth	1	21	21.0	21	0
Rogers, J.	1	16	16.0	16	0
Brock	1	12	12.0	12	0
TOTAL	4	70	17.5	21	0

Fumbles	No	Own Rec	Own Yds	Own TD	Opp Rec	Opp Yds	Opp TD	OB
Rogers, G.	1	0	0	0	0	0	0	0
Wilson, D.	1	0	0	0	0	0	0	0
Myers	1	1	0	0	0	0	0	0
Nairne	0	0	0	0	1	0	0	0
TOTAL	3	1	0	0	1	0	0	0

GAME SUMMARY

Visitor: San Francisco 49ers   **vs.**   **Home:** Washington Redskins
Date: 4 October 1981   **At:** RFK Stadium
Day of Week: Sunday   **Starting Time:** 1:01 P.M.
Weather: Sunny
Temperature: 65°F   **Wind and Direction:** WSW 10 mph
ATTENDANCE:
Tickets Distributed: 55,045   **Actual:** 51,843   **Time:** 3:05

SCORING BY QUARTER

	1	2	3	4	OT	TOTAL
San Francisco 49ers	14	10	6	0		30
Redskins	0	3	0	14		17

SCORING BY PLAY AND DRIVE

Team	Per.	Elapsed Time	Scoring Play	Vis.	Home
SF	1	5:38	Patton yd run (Bahr kick)	7	0
SF	1	10:44	Hicks 80 fumble (Bahr kick)	14	0
SF	2	2:39	Bahr 43 FG	17	0
WA	2	6:14	Moseley 34 FG	17	3
SF	2	8:43	Davis 1 run (Bahr kick)	24	3
SF	3	9:09	Hicks 32 interception	30	3
WA	4	4:27	Nelms 58 punt return (Moseley kick)	30	10
WA	4	10:12	Washington 5 run (Moseley kick)	30	17

FINAL TEAM STATISTICS

	49ERS	REDSKINS
Total first downs	16	19
By rushing	6	6
By passing	9	11
By penalty	1	2
Third down efficiency	6/15–40%	8/16–50%
Total net yards	296	304
Total offensive plays*	65	67
Average gain per offensive play	4.6	4.5
Net yards rushing	128	83
Total rushing plays	35	23
Average gain per rushing play	3.7	3.6
Net yards passing	168	221
Times thrown/yds. lost att. to pass	2/25	2/20
Gross yards passing	193	241
Pass atts./completions/had intercepted	28/15/1	46/22/4
Avg. gain per pass play*	5.6	4.6
Punts—number/average	5/40.0	5/40.4
Had blocked	0	0
Total return yardage	176	224
Number/yards punt returns	2/9	2/59
Number/yards kickoff returns	2/41	6/162
Number/yards interception returns	4/126	1/3
Penalties—number/yards	3/27	7/50
Fumbles—number/lost	1/1	4/2
Touchdowns	4	2
Rushing	2	1
Passing	0	0
Returns	2	1
Extra points made/attempts	3/3	2/2
Field goals made/attempts	1/2	1/1
Time of possession	29:17	30:43

*Includes times thrown passing

INDIVIDUAL TEAM STATISTICS

San Francisco 49ers

Rushing	Att	Yds	Avg	LG	TD
Patton	9	43		16	1
Cooper	6	21		12	0
Davis	13	37		5	1
Elliott	3	12		7	0
Easley	2	1		1	0
Lawrence	2	14		8	0
TOTAL	35	128		16	2

Passing	Att	Cp	Yds	TD	LG	Int	Tk/Yds
Montana	28	15	193	0	40	1	2/25
TOTAL	28	15	193	0	40	1	2/25

Receiving	No	Yds	LG	TD
Clark	1	21	21	0
Young	2	24	19	0
Solomon	5	77	40	0
Elliott	6	69	19	0
Cooper	1	2	2	0
TOTAL	15	193	40	0

Interceptions	No	Yds	Avg	LG	TD
Hicks	2	104		72	1
Lott	1	0		0	0
McColl	1	22		22	0
TOTAL	4	126		72	1

Punting	No	Yds	Avg	TB	In 20	LP
Miller	5	200	40.0	1	1	53
TOTAL	5	200	40.0	1	1	53

Punt Returns	No	FC	Yds	Avg	LG	TD
Solomon	2	1	9		13	0
Hicks	0	1	0		0	0
TOTAL	2	2	9		13	0

Kickoff Rets	No	Yds	Avg	LG	TD
Lawrence	2	41		21	0
TOTAL	2	41		21	0

Fumbles	No	Own Rec	Own Yds	Own TD	Opp Rec	Opp Yds	Opp TD	OB
Hicks	0	0	0	0	1	80	1	0
Stuckey	0	0	0	0	1	0	0	0
Elliott	1	0	0	0	0	0	0	0
TOTAL	1	0	0	0	2	80	1	0

Washington Redskins

Rushing	Att	Yds	Avg	LG	TD
Riggins	13	47		8	0
Metcalf	2	5		3	0
Washington	7	30		7	1
Theismann	1	1		1	0
TOTAL	23	83		8	1

Passing	Att	Cp	Yds	TD	LG	Int	Tk/Yds
Theismann	24	10	123	0	33	2	1/11
Flick	22	12	118	0	33	2	1/9
TOTAL	46	22	241	0	33	4	2/20

Receiving	No	Yds	LG	TD
Monk	4	42	13	0
Metcalf	3	44	33	0
Walker	2	29	23	0
Harmon	1	11	11	0
McCrary	1	12	12	0
Washington	8	49	18	0
Thompson	2	42	33	0
Warren	1	12	12	0
TOTAL	22	241	33	0

Interceptions	No	Yds	Avg	LG	TD
Nelms	1	3		3	0
TOTAL	1	3		3	0

Punting	No	Yds	Avg	TB	In 20	Lp
Connell	5	202	40.4	0	2	57
TOTAL	5	202	40.4	0	2	57

Punt Returns	No	FC	Yds	Avg	LG	TD
Nelms	2	0	59		58	1
TOTAL	2	0	59		58	1

Kickoff Rets	No	Yds	Avg	LG	TD
Nelms	4	123		55	0
Seay	1	19		19	0
Wonsley	1	20		20	0
TOTAL	6	162		55	0

Fumbles	No	Own Rec	Own Yds	Own TD	Opp Rec	Opp Yds	Opp TD	OB
Metcalf	1	0	0	0	0	0	0	0
Washington	1	0	0	0	0	0	0	0
Milot	1	0	0	0	1	18	0	0
Peters	0	1	0	0	0	0	0	0
Flick	1	1	0	0	0	0	0	0
TOTAL	4	2	0	0	1	18	0	0

GAME SUMMARY

Visitor: Dallas Cowboys vs. **Home:** San Francisco 49ers
Date: 11 October 1981   **At:** Candlestick Park, SF
Day of Week: Sunday   **Starting Time:** 1:01 P.M.
Weather: Sunny with fleecy clouds
Temperature: 62°F   **Wind and Direction:** NW 18–21 mph
ATTENDANCE:
Tickets Distributed: 61,127   **Actual:** 57,574   **Time:** 3:10

SCORING BY QUARTER

	1	2	3	4	OT	TOTAL
Dallas Cowboys	0	7	0	7		14
San Francisco 49ers	21	3	14	7		45

SCORING BY PLAY AND DRIVE

Team	Per.	Elapsed Time	Scoring Play	Vis.	Home
SF	1	3:45	Solomon 1 pass from Montana (Wersching kick)—61 yards, 11 plays	0	7
SF	1	7:53	Hofer 4 run (Wersching kick)—68 yards, 6 plays	0	14
SF	1	13:46	Davis 1 run (Wersching kick)—6 yards, 4 plays	0	21
SF	2	1:26	Wersching FG 18—32 yards, 7 plays	0	24
DS	2	11:01	Hill 22 pass from Pearson (Septien kick)—86 yards, 10 plays	7	24
SF	3	5:48	Clark 78 pass from Montana (Wersching kick)—78 yards, 1 play	7	31
SF	3	6:23	Lott 41 interception return (Wersching kick)	7	38
SF	4	2:07	Lawrence 1 run (Wersching kick)—89 yards, 16 plays	7	45
DS	4	6:53	Barnes 72 fumble return (Septien kick)	14	45

FINAL TEAM STATISTICS

	DALLAS	49ERS
Total first downs	10	23
By rushing	4	8
By passing	5	14
By penalty	1	1
Third down efficiency	3/13–23.1%	9/18–50.0%
Total net yards	192	440
Total offensive plays*	53	80
Average gain per offensive play	3.6	5.5
Net yards rushing	83	150
Total rushing plays	21	46
Average gain per rushing play	4.0	3.3
Net yards passing	109	290
Times thrown/yds. lost att. to pass	3/26	1/14
Gross yards passing	135	304
Pass atts./completions/had intercepted	29/12/2	33/20/0
Avg. gain per pass play*	3.4	8.5
Punts—number/average	8/39.5	6/46.2
Had blocked	0	0
Total return yardage	210	110
Number/yards punt returns	3/2	3/8
Number/yards kickoff returns	8/136	2/40
Number/yards interception returns	0/0	2/53
Penalties—number/yards	5/40	4/28
Fumbles—number/lost	3/2	4/1
Touchdowns	2	6
Rushing	0	3
Passing	1	2
Returns	1	1
Extra points made/attempts	2/2	6/6
Field goals made/attempts	0/0	1/2
Time of possession	25:53	34:07

*Includes times thrown passing

INDIVIDUAL TEAM STATISTICS

Dallas Cowboys

Rushing	Att	Yds	Avg	LG	TD
Jones, J.	4	26	6.5	16	0
Dorsett	9	21	2.3	7	0
Cosbie	1	15	15.0	15	0
Springs	5	14	2.8	7	0
White, D.	1	7	7.0	7	0
Carano	1	0	0.0	0	0
TOTAL	21	83	4.0	16	0

Passing	Att	Cp	Yds	TD	LG	Int	Tk/Yds
White, D.	16	8	60	0	16	2	3/26
Carano	12	3	53	0	21	0	0/0
Pearson	1	1	22	1	22	0	0/0
TOTAL	29	12	135	1	22	2	3/26

Receiving	No	Yds	LG	TD
Springs	3	9	7	0
Donley	2	26	17	0
Pearson	2	23	16	0
Hill	1	22	22	1
Newhouse	1	21	21	0
Cosbie	1	15	15	0
Dorsett	1	14	14	0
DuPree	1	5	5	0
TOTAL	12	135	22	1

Interceptions	No	Yds	Avg	LG	TD
TOTAL	0	0	0.0	0	0

Punting	No	Yds	Avg	TB	In 20	LP
White, D.	8	316	39.5	0	0	47
TOTAL	8	316	39.5	0	0	47

Punt Returns	No	FC	Yds	Avg	LG	TD
Fellows	2	1	3	1.5	2	0
Jones, J.	1	0	−1	−1.0	−1	0
TOTAL	3	1	2	0.7	2	0

Kickoff Rets	No	Yds	Avg	LG	TD
Jones, J.	2	49	24.5	28	0
Fellows	2	46	23.0	26	0
Newsome	2	22	11.0	17	0
Newhouse	2	19	9.5	12	0
TOTAL	8	136	17.0	28	0

Fumbles	No	Own Rec	Yds	TD	Opp Rec	Yds	TD	OB
White, D.	1	0	0	0	0	0	0	0
Pearson	1	0	0	0	0	0	0	0
Carano	1	0	0	0	0	0	0	0
Rafferty	0	1	0	0	0	0	0	0
Barnes	0	0	0	0	1	72	0	0
TOTAL	3	1	0	0	1	72	0	0

San Francisco 49ers

Rushing	Att	Yds	Avg	LG	TD
Hofer	11	40	3.6	12	1
Davis	8	28	3.5	6	1
Easley	8	28	3.5	8	0
Lawrence	6	27	4.5	14	1
Patton	7	16	2.3	7	0
Cooper	5	9	1.8	5	0
Montana	1	2	2.0	2	0
TOTAL	46	150	3.3	14	3

Passing	Att	Cp	Yds	TD	LG	Int	Tk/Yds
Montana	29	19	279	2	78	0	0/0
Solomon	1	1	25	0	25	0	0/0
Benjamin	3	0	0	0	0	0	1/14
TOTAL	33	20	304	2	78	0	1/14

Receiving	No	Yds	LG	TD
Solomon	5	74	26	1
Clark	4	135	78	1
Young	3	35	12	0
Hofer	3	22	12	0
Wilson	2	22	11	0
Cooper	2	12	6	0
Patton	1	4	4	0
TOTAL	20	304	78	2

Interceptions	No	Yds	Avg	LG	TD
Lott	2	53	26.5	41	1
TOTAL	2	53	26.5	41	1

Punting	No	Yds	Avg	TB	In 20	LP
Miller	6	277	46.2	1	2	55
TOTAL	6	277	46.2	1	2	55

Punt Returns	No	FC	Yds	Avg	LG	TD
Solomon	2	1	5	2.5	5	0
Hicks	1	0	3	3.0	3	0
TOTAL	3	1	8	2.7	5	0

Kickoff Rets	No	Yds	Avg	LG	TD
Lawrence	2	49	24.5	30	0
TOTAL	2	49	24.5	30	0

Fumbles	No	Own Rec	Yds	TD	Opp Rec	Yds	TD	OB
Lawrence	2	0	0	0	0	0	0	0
Cooper	2	1	0	0	0	0	0	0
Wilson	0	1	0	0	0	0	0	0
Lott	0	0	0	0	1	0	0	0
Solomon	0	1	0	0	0	0	0	0
Turner	0	0	0	0	1	0	0	0
TOTAL	4	3	0	0	2	0	0	0

GAME SUMMARY

Visitor: San Francisco 49ers   **vs.**   **Home:** Green Bay Packers
Date: 18 October 1981   **At:** Milwaukee, Wis.
Day of Week: Sunday   **Starting Time:** 12:03 P.M.
Weather: Occasional showers with possible snow
Temperature: 40°F   **Wind and Direction:** W 23 mph
ATTENDANCE:
Tickets Distributed: 55,950   **Actual:** 50,171   **Time:** 2:50

SCORING BY QUARTER

	1	2	3	4	OT	TOTAL
San Francisco 49ers	0	3	7	3		13
Green Bay Packers	0	3	0	0		3

SCORING BY PLAY AND DRIVE

Team	Per.	Elapsed Time	Scoring Play	Vis.	Home
GB	2	1:26	Stenerud 26 yd FG	0	3
SF	2	14:57	Wersching 26 yd FG	3	3
SF	3	11:49	Davis 1 yd TD (Wersching kick)	10	3
SF	4	10:29	Wersching 32 yd FG	13	3

FINAL TEAM STATISTICS

	49ERS	PACKERS
Total first downs	21	13
By rushing	10	4
By passing	11	9
By penalty	0	0
Third down efficiency	10/21–48%	0/10–0%
Total net yards	326	243
Total offensive plays*	80	47
Average gain per offensive play	4.1	6.2
Net yards rushing	126	78
Total rushing plays	47	19
Average gain per rushing play	2.7	4.1
Net yards passing	201	165
Times thrown/yds. lost att. to pass	1/9	4/30
Gross yards passing	210	193
Pass atts./completions/had intercepted	32/23/0	24/14/0
Avg. gain per pass play*	6.1	6.9
Punts—number/average	7/35.9	7/40.0
Had blocked	0	0
Total return yardage	85	101
Number/yards punt returns	4/38	2/5
Number/yards kickoff returns	1/21	3/96
Number/yards interception returns	1/26	0/0
Penalties—number/yards	7/35	4/35
Fumbles—number/lost	2/1	1/0
Touchdowns	1	0
Rushing	1	0
Passing	0	0
Returns	0	0
Extra points made/attempts	1/1	0/0
Field goals made/attempts	2/2	1/2
Time of possession	37:41	22:19

*Includes times thrown passing

INDIVIDUAL TEAM STATISTICS

Green Bay Packers

Rushing	Att	Yds	Avg	LG	TD
Huckleby	10	20	2.0	12	0
Ellis	7	50	7.1	23	0
Dickey	1	0	0.0	0	0
Whitehurst	1	8	8.0	8	0
TOTAL	19	78	4.1	23	0

Passing	Att	Cp	Yds	TD	LG	Int	Tk/Yds
Dickey	18	11	156	0	28	0	3/28
Whitehurst	6	3	37	0	19	1	1/2
TOTAL	24	14	193	0	28	1	4/30

Receiving	No	Yds	LG	TD
Ellis	5	50	28	0
Lofton	1	13	13	0
Coffman	3	67	27	0
Huckleby	1	0	0	0
Jefferson	3	47	18	0
Jensen	1	16	16	0
TOTAL	14	193	28	0

Interceptions	No	Yds	Avg	LG	TD
TOTAL	0	0	0.0	0	0

Punting	No	Yds	Avg	TB	In 20	LP
Stachowicz	7	280	40.0	0	1	55
TOTAL	7	280	40.0	0	1	55

Punt Returns	No	FC	Yds	Avg	LG	TD
Lee	2	0	5		5	0
Grey	1	0	0		0	0
TOTAL	3	0	5		5	0

Kickoff Rets	No	Yds	Avg	LG	TD
Lee	2	44		24	0
Coffman	1	52		52	0
TOTAL	3	96		52	0

Fumbles	No	Own Rec	Yds	TD	Opp Rec	Yds	TD	OB
Douglass	0	1	0	0	0	0	0	0
Dickey	1	1	−7	0	0	0	0	0
TOTAL	1	2	−7	0	0	0	0	0

San Francisco 49ers

Rushing	Att	Yds	Avg	LG	TD
Davis	15	64	4.3	14	0
Cooper	14	41	2.9	7	1
Patton	6	12	2.2	6	0
Hofer	8	3	0.4	8	0
Montana	1	2	2.0	2	0
Easley	3	3	1.0	2	0
TOTAL	47	126	2.7	14	1

Passing	Att	Cp	Yds	TD	LG	Int	Tk/Yds
Montana	32	23	210	0	22	0	1/9
TOTAL	32	23	210	0	22	0	1/9

Receiving	No	Yds	LG	TD
Davis	1	3	3	0
Solomon	4	49	17	0
Hofer	5	44	22	0
Patton	3	31	19	0
Cooper	2	19	13	0
Clark	6	55	12	0
Young	1	4	4	0
Lawrence	1	5	5	0
TOTAL	23	210	22	0

Interceptions	No	Yds	Avg	LG	TD
Hicks	1	26	26	1	1
TOTAL	1	26	26	1	1

Punting	No	Yds	Avg	TB	In 20	LP
Miller	7	251	35.9	1	3	56
TOTAL	7	251	35.9	1	3	56

Punt Returns	No	FC	Yds	Avg	LG	TD
Solomon	3	0	24		14	0
Hicks	1	0	14		14	0
TOTAL	4	0	38		14	0

Kickoff Rets	No	Yds	Avg	LG	TD
Lawrence	2	21		21	0
TOTAL	2	21		21	0

Fumbles	No	Own Rec	Own Yds	Own TD	Opp Rec	Opp Yds	Opp TD	OB
Davis	1	0	0	0	0	0	0	0
Easley	1	1	0	0	0	0	0	0
TOTAL	2	1	0	0	0	0	0	0

GAME SUMMARY

Visitor: Los Angeles Rams   **vs.**   **Home:** San Francisco 49ers
Date: 25 October 1981   **At:** Candlestick Park, SF
Day of Week: Sunday   **Starting Time:** 1:02 P.M.
Weather: Partly cloudy, intermittently sunny
Temperature: 63°F   **Wind and Direction:** N to NW, 10–15 mph

ATTENDANCE:
Tickets Distributed: 61,113   **Actual:** 59,190   **Time:** 3:14

SCORING BY QUARTER

	1	2	3	4	OT	TOTAL
Los Angeles Rams	0	10	7	0		17
San Francisco 49ers	14	3	3	0		20

SCORING BY PLAY AND DRIVE

Team	Per.	Elapsed Time	Scoring Play	Score Vis.	Home
SF	1	9:38	Solomon 14 pass from Montana (Wersching kick)—68 yards, 9 plays	0	7
SF	1	14:59	Clark 41 pass from Montana (Wersching kick)—53 yards, 3 plays	0	14
LA	2	7:22	Corral FG 25—34 yards, 10 plays	3	14
LA	2	13:57	Guman 2 run (Corral kick)—96 yards, 16 plays	10	14
SF	2	15:00	Wersching FG 42—53 yards, 5 plays	10	17
SF	3	12:01	Wersching FG 18—79 yards, 14 plays	10	20
LA	3	14:04	Tyler 16 pass from Haden (Corral kick)—66 yards, 5 plays	17	20

FINAL TEAM STATISTICS

	RAMS	49ERS
Total first downs	25	14
By rushing	9	3
By passing	13	10
By penalty	3	1
Third down efficiency	7/22–31.8%	3/14–21.4%
Total net yards	401	325
Total offensive plays*	82	63
Average gain per offensive play	4.9	5.2
Net yards rushing	145	60
Total rushing plays	37	28
Average gain per rushing play	3.9	2.1
Net yards passing	256	265
Times thrown/yds. lost att. to pass	6/54	3/22
Gross yards passing	310	287
Pass atts./completions/had intercepted	39/20/1	32/18/0
Avg. gain per pass play*	5.7	7.6
Punts—number/average	5/43.0	10/43.3
Had blocked	0	0
Total return yardage	267	90
Number/yards punt returns	8/166	2/9
Number/yards kickoff returns	4/101	4/81
Number/yards interception returns	0/0	1/0
Penalties—number/yards	7/39	5/45
Fumbles—number/lost	0/0	0/0
Touchdowns	2	2
Rushing	1	0
Passing	1	2
Returns	0	0
Extra points made/attempts	2/2	2/2
Field goals made/attempts	1/5	2/2
Time of possession	33:18	26:42

*Includes times thrown passing

INDIVIDUAL TEAM STATISTICS

Los Angeles Rams

Rushing	Att	Yds	Avg	LG	TD
Tyler	22	90	4.1	18	0
Guman	7	34	4.9	15	1
Bryant	7	13	1.9	5	0
Haden	1	8	8.0	8	0
TOTAL	37	145	3.9	18	1

Passing	Att	Cp	Yds	TD	LG	Int	Tk/Yds
Haden	39	20	310	1	39	1	6/54
TOTAL	39	20	310	1	39	1	6/54

Receiving	No	Yds	LG	TD
Dennard	6	119	34	0
Tyler	4	55	21	1
Waddy	4	52	19	0
Arnold	3	19	12	0
Bryant	1	39	39	0
Hill, D.	1	13	13	0
Guman	1	13	13	0
TOTAL	20	310	39	1

Interceptions	No	Yds	Avg	LG	TD
TOTAL	0	0	0.0	0	0

Punting	No	Yds	Avg	TB	In 20	LP
Corral	5	215	43.0	2	1	47
TOTAL	5	215	43.0	2	1	47

Punt Returns	No	FC	Yds	Avg	LG	TD
Irvin	7	1	127	18.1	46	0
Johnson	1	0	39	39.0	39	0
TOTAL	8	1	166	20.8	46	0

Kickoff Rets	No	Yds	Avg	LG	TD
Hill, D.	3	79	26.3	27	0
Sully	1	22	22.0	22	0
TOTAL	4	101	25.3	27	0

Fumbles	No	Own Rec	Yds	TD	Opp Rec	Yds	TD	OB
TOTAL	0	0	0	0	0	0	0	0

San Francisco 49ers

Rushing	Att	Yds	Avg	LG	TD
Hofer	8	23	2.9	11	0
Davis	6	14	2.3	4	0
Patton	6	13	2.2	9	0
Cooper	5	7	1.4	3	0
Montana	2	3	1.5	5	0
Easley	1	0	0.0	0	0
TOTAL	28	60	2.1	11	0

Passing	Att	Cp	Yds	TD	LG	Int	Tk/Yds
Montana	32	18	287	2	50	0	3/22
TOTAL	32	18	287	2	50	0	3/22

Receiving	No	Yds	LG	TD
Clark	8	109	41	1
Solomon	5	79	40	1
Cooper	2	57	50	0
Young	1	29	29	0
Patton	1	8	8	0
Wilson	1	5	5	0
TOTAL	18	287	50	2

Interceptions	No	Yds	Avg	LG	TD
Lott	1	0	0.0	0	0
TOTAL	1	0	0.0	0	0

Punting	No	Yds	Avg	TB	In 20	LP
Miller	10	433	43.3	1	0	54
TOTAL	10	433	43.3	1	0	54

Punt Returns	No	FC	Yds	Avg	LG	TD
Solomon	2	0	9	4.5	5	0
TOTAL	2	0	9	4.5	5	0

Kickoff Rets	No	Yds	Avg	LG	TD
Lawrence	2	61	30.5	38	0
Ramson	1	12	12.0	12	0
Wilson	1	8	8.0	8	0
TOTAL	4	81	20.3	38	0

Fumbles	No	Own Rec	Own Yds	TD	Opp Rec	Opp Yds	TD	OB
TOTAL	0	0	0	0	0	0	0	0

GAME SUMMARY

Visitor: San Francisco 49ers   **vs.**   **Home:** Pittsburgh Steelers
Date: 1 November 1981   **At:** 3 Rivers Stadium
Day of Week: Sunday   **Starting Time:** 1:02 P.M.
Weather: Partly sunny
Temperature: 60°F   **Wind and Direction:** S 6 mph
ATTENDANCE:
Tickets Distributed: **Actual:** 52,878   **Time:** 2:55

SCORING BY QUARTER

	1	2	3	4	OT	TOTAL
San Francisco 49ers	0	10	0	7		17
Steelers	0	0	14	0		14

SCORING BY PLAY AND DRIVE

Team	Per.	Elapsed Time	Scoring Play	Vis.	Home
SF	2	14:28	Young 5 pass from Montana (Wersching kick) (8–46)	7	0
SF	2	14:57	Wersching FG 45 (2–9)	10	0
PT	3	4:24	Blount 50 on pass interception (Trout kick) (0–0)	10	7
PT	3	8:21	Smith 22 pass from Bradshaw (Trout kick) (1–22)	10	14
SF	4	9:25	Easley 1 run (Wersching kick) (9–43)	17	14

FINAL TEAM STATISTICS

	49ERS	STEELERS
Total first downs	25	16
By rushing	10	7
By passing	10	8
By penalty	5	1
Third down efficiency	7/16–43.8%	5/8–62.5%
Total net yards	330	269
Total offensive plays*	78	51
Average gain per offensive play	4.2	5.3
Net yards rushing	130	144
Total rushing plays	39	28
Average gain per rushing play	3.3	5.5
Net yards passing	200	125
Times thrown/yds. lost att. to pass	1/10	0/0
Gross yards passing	210	125
Pass atts./completions/had intercepted	38/23/2	23/12/3
Avg. gain per pass play*	5.1	5.0
Punts—number/average	5/45.8	2/48.5
Had blocked	0	0
Total return yardage	83	192
Number/yards punt returns	0/0	4/41
Number/yards kickoff returns	3/58	4/70
Number/yards interception returns	3/28	2/81
Penalties—number/yards	6/55	8/45
Fumbles—number/lost	0/0	3/3
Touchdowns	2	2
Rushing	1	0
Passing	1	1
Returns	0	1
Extra points made/attempts	2/2	2/2
Field goals made/attempts	1/2	0/0
Time of possession	34:16	25:44

*Includes times thrown passing

INDIVIDUAL TEAM STATISTICS

Pittsburgh Steelers

Rushing	Att	Yds	Avg	LG	TD
Harris	17	104	6.3	21	0
Pollard	7	28	4.0	7	0
Bradshaw	3	7	5.5	8	0
Davis	1	5	5.0	5	0
TOTAL	28	144	5.5	21	0

Passing	Att	Cp	Yds	TD	LG	Int	Tk/Yds
Bradshaw	23	12	125	1	26	3	0/0
TOTAL	23	12	125	1	26	3	0/0

Receiving	No	Yds	LG	TD
Stallworth	3	26	12	0
Cunningham	2	9	5	0
Harris	1	8	8	0
Pollard	3	42	26	0
Smith	2	42	22	1
Grossman	1	−2	−2	0
TOTAL	12	125	26	1

Interceptions	No	Yds	Avg	LG	TD
Blount	1	50		50	1
Lambert	1	31		31	0
TOTAL	2	81		50	1

Punting	No	Yds	Avg	TB	In 20	LP
Colquitt	2	97	48.5	1	1	50
TOTAL	2	97	48.5	1	1	50

Punt Returns	No	FC	Yds	Avg	LG	TD
Smith	4	1	41		17	0
TOTAL	4	1	41		17	0

Kickoff Rets	No	Yds	Avg	LG	TD
Hawthorne	3	69		30	0
Thornton	1	1		1	0
TOTAL	4	70		30	0

Fumbles	No	Own Rec	Yds	TD	Opp Rec	Yds	TD	OB
Harris	1	0	0	0	0	0	0	0
Pollard	2	0	0	0	0	0	0	0
TOTAL	3	0	0	0	0	0	0	0

San Francisco 49ers

Rushing	Att	Yds	Avg	LG	TD
Patton	13	35	2.7	9	0
Cooper	3	10	3.3	6	0
Easley	14	47	3.4	7	1
Hofer	5	26	5.2	12	0
Montana	4	12	3.0	8	0
TOTAL	39	130	3.3	12	1

Passing	Att	Cp	Yds	TD	LG	Int	Tk/Yds
Montana	37	22	205	1	23	2	1/10
Easley	1	1	5	0	5	0	0/0
TOTAL	38	23	210	1	23	2	1/10

Receiving	No	Yds	LG	TD
Cooper	5	53	22	0
Clark	7	80	23	0
Easley	3	12	6	0
Patton	2	17	10	0
Solomon	2	33	23	0
Young	3	13	5	1
Hofer	1	2	2	0
TOTAL	23	210	23	1

Interceptions	No	Yds	Avg	LG	TD
Wright	1	0		0	0
Hicks	1	0		0	0
Williamson	1	28		28	0
TOTAL	3	28		28	0

Punting	No	Yds	Avg	TB	In 20	LP
Miller	5	229	45.8	0	1	55
TOTAL	5	229	45.8	0	1	55

Punt Returns	No	FC	Yds	Avg	LG	TD
TOTAL	0	0	0		0	0

Kickoff Rets	No	Yds	Avg	LG	TD
Wilson	2	37		21	0
Ring	1	21		21	0
TOTAL	3	58		21	0

Fumbles	No	Own Rec	Yds	TD	Opp Rec	Yds	TD	OB
Wright	0	0	0	0	1	0	0	0
Williamson	0	0	0	0	1	0	0	0
Lott	0	0	0	0	1	0	0	0
TOTAL	0	0	0	0	3	0	0	0

GAME SUMMARY

Visitor: Atlanta Falcons   **vs.**   **Home:** San Francisco 49ers
Date: 8 November 1981   **At:** Candlestick Park, SF
Day of Week: Sunday   **Starting Time:** 1:01 P.M.
Weather: Hazy overcast skies; relative humidity 78%
Temperature: 61°F   **Wind and Direction:** Variable to 5 mph

ATTENDANCE:
Tickets Distributed: 61,118   **Actual:** 59,127   **Time:** 3:20

SCORING BY QUARTER

	1	2	3	4	OT	TOTAL
Atlanta Falcons	0	0	7	7		14
San Francisco 49ers	0	10	0	7		17

SCORING BY PLAY AND DRIVE

Team	Per.	Elapsed Time	Scoring Play	Vis.	Home
SF	2	11:08	Solomon 14 pass from Montana (72 yards, 2 plays)— (Wersching kick)	0	7
SF	2	15:00	Wersching FG 48 (24 yards, 2 plays)	0	10
ATL	3	10:40	Andrews 1 run (75 yards, 16 plays)— (Luckhurst kick)	7	10
SF	4	7:31	Young 3 pass from Montana (77 yards, 13 plays)— (Wersching kick)	7	17
ATL	4	13:17	Jackson 25 pass from Bartkowski (76 yards, 6 plays)— (Luckhurst kick)	14	17

FINAL TEAM STATISTICS

	FALCONS	49ERS
Total first downs	19	17
By rushing	4	4
By passing	13	11
By penalty	2	2
Third down efficiency	5/15–33.3%	8/19–42.1%
Total net yards	292	287
Total offensive plays*	71	66
Average gain per offensive play	4.1	4.3
Net yards rushing	76	82
Total rushing plays	26	34
Average gain per rushing play	2.9	2.4
Net yards passing	216	205
Times thrown/yds. lost att. to pass	3/20	2/18
Gross yards passing	236	223
Pass atts./completions/had intercepted	42/20/3	30/16/1
Avg. gain per pass play*	4.8	6.4
Punts—number/average	8/44.9	10/42.0
Had blocked	0	0
Total return yardage	126	139
Number/yards punt returns	5/36	7/51
Number/yards kickoff returns	3/67	2/51
Number/yards interception returns	1/23	3/37
Penalties—number/yards	8/82	10/69
Fumbles—number/lost	2/0	4/0
Touchdowns	2	2
Rushing	1	0
Passing	1	2
Returns	0	0
Extra points made/attempts	2/2	2/2
Field goals made/attempts	0/1	1/1
Time of possession	29:29	30:31

*Includes times thrown passing

INDIVIDUAL TEAM STATISTICS

Atlanta Falcons

Rushing	Att	Yds	Avg	LG	TD
Andrews	18	61	3.4	14	1
Cain	5	10	2.0	12	0
Jackson	1	5	5.0	5	0
Bartkowski	2	0	0.0	0	0
TOTAL	26	76	2.9	14	1

Passing	Att	Cp	Yds	TD	LG	Int	Tk/Yds
Bartkowski	42	20	236	1	31	3	3/20
TOTAL	42	20	236	1	31	3	3/20

Receiving	No	Yds	LG	TD
Jenkins	7	134	31	0
Andrews	6	31	10	0
Cain	4	24	8	0
Jackson	2	35	25	1
Miller	1	12	12	0
TOTAL	20	236	31	1

Interceptions	No	Yds	Avg	LG	TD
Johnson	1	23	23.0	23	0
TOTAL	1	23	23.0	23	0

Punting	No	Yds	Avg	TB	In 20	LP
James	8	359	44.9	0	1	53
TOTAL	8	359	44.9	0	1	53

Punt Returns	No	FC	Yds	Avg	LG	TD
Woerner	2	1	20	10.0	13	0
Johnson	2	0	8	4.0	4	0
Smith, R.	1	0	8	8.0	8	0
TOTAL	5	1	36	7.2	13	0

Kickoff Rets	No	Yds	Avg	LG	TD
Woerner	2	41	20.5	22	0
Smith, R.	1	26	26.0	26	0
TOTAL	3	67	22.3	26	0

Fumbles	No	Own Rec	Own Yds	Own TD	Opp Rec	Opp Yds	Opp TD	OB
Bartkowski	2	1	0	0	0	0	0	0
Van Note	0	1	0	0	0	0	0	0
TOTAL	2	2	0	0	0	0	0	0

San Francisco 49ers

Rushing	Att	Yds	Avg	LG	TD
Easley	15	31	2.1	7	0
Patton	9	26	2.9	7	0
Solomon	3	11	3.7	7	0
Clark	1	9	9.0	9	0
Cooper	3	4	1.3	6	0
Montana	2	1	0.5	1	0
Hofer	1	0	0.0	0	0
TOTAL	34	82	2.4	9	0

Passing	Att	Cp	Yds	TD	LG	Int	Tk/Yds
Montana	30	16	223	2	44	1	2/18
TOTAL	30	16	223	2	44	1	2/18

Receiving	No	Yds	LG	TD
Clark	7	128	44	0
Solomon	3	56	24	1
Easley	2	9	6	0
Young	2	9	6	1
Hofer	1	21	21	0
Cooper	1	0	0	0
TOTAL	16	223	44	2

Interceptions	No	Yds	Avg	LG	TD
Hicks	2	37	18.5	20	0
Martin	1	0	0.0	0	0
TOTAL	3	37	12.3	20	0

Punting	No	Yds	Avg	TB	In 20	LP
Miller	10	420	42.0	1	2	53
TOTAL	10	420	42.0	1	2	53

Punt Returns	No	FC	Yds	Avg	LG	TD
Hicks	4	1	36	9.0	15	0
Solomon	3	0	15	5.0	11	0
Montana	1	0	8	8.0	8	0
TOTAL	8	1	59	7.4	15	0

Kickoff Rets	No	Yds	Avg	LG	TD
Ring	1	29	29.0	29	0
Hicks	1	22	22.0	22	0
TOTAL	2	51	25.5	29	0

Fumbles	No	Own Rec	Yds	TD	Opp Rec	Yds	TD	OB
Hicks	1	1	0	0	0	0	0	0
Solomon	1	1	0	0	0	0	0	0
Patton	1	0	0	0	0	0	0	0
Easley	1	1	0	0	0	0	0	0
Fahnhorst	0	1	0	0	0	0	0	0
TOTAL	4	4	0	0	0	0	0	0

GAME SUMMARY

Visitor: Cleveland Browns **vs.** **Home:** San Francisco 49ers
Date: 15 November 1981 **At:** Candlestick Park, SF
Day of Week: Sunday **Starting Time:** 1:01 P.M.
Weather: Very overcast, rain falling at kickoff, soggy field
Temperature: 62°F **Wind and Direction:** S 15 mph
ATTENDANCE:
Tickets Distributed: 60,952 **Actual:** 52,445 **Time:** 3:15

SCORING BY QUARTER

	1	2	3	4	OT	TOTAL
Cleveland Browns	2	3	0	10		15
San Francisco 49ers	0	6	6	0		12

SCORING BY PLAY AND DRIVE

Team	Per.	Elapsed Time	Scoring Play	Score Vis.	Home
CL	1	6:25	Harris tackled Montana in end zone (int. grounding)	2	0
SF	2	3:32	Wersching FG 28 (70 yards, 14 plays)	2	3
CL	2	7:48	Bahr FG 28 (69 yards, 11 plays)	5	3
SF	2	13:53	Wersching FG 29 (50 yards, 15 plays)	5	6
SF	3	6:36	Wersching FG 28 (45 yards, 12 plays)	5	9
SF	3	14:00	Wersching FG 28 (51 yards, 12 plays)	5	12
CL	4	8:14	Rucker 21 pass from Sipe (Bahr kick)—43 yards, 6 plays	12	12
CL	4	14:17	Bahr FG 24 (59 yards, 11 plays)	15	12

FINAL TEAM STATISTICS

	BROWNS	49ERS
Total first downs	14	21
By rushing	5	8
By passing	9	12
By penalty	0	1
Third down efficiency	7/17–41.2%	9/20–45.0%
Total net yards	267	305
Total offensive plays*	61	80
Average gain per offensive play	4.4	3.8
Net yards rushing	106	118
Total rushing plays	26	35
Average gain per rushing play	4.1	3.4
Net yards passing	161	187
Times thrown/yds. lost att. to pass	2/19	3/26
Gross yards passing	180	213
Pass atts./completions/had intercepted	33/16/1	42/24/2
Avg. gain per pass play*	4.6	4.2
Punts—number/average	5/42.4	4/36.0
Had blocked	0	0
Total return yardage	165	84
Number/yards punt returns	3/50	2/22
Number/yards kickoff returns	3/82	2/52
Number/yards interception returns	2/33	1/10
Penalties—number/yards	7/55	4/29
Fumbles—number/lost	1/1	1/0
Touchdowns	1	0
Rushing	0	0
Passing	1	0
Returns	0	0
Extra points made/attempts	1/1	0/0
Field goals made/attempts	2/3	4/5
Time of possession	24:48	35:12

*Includes times thrown passing

INDIVIDUAL TEAM STATISTICS

Cleveland Browns

Rushing	Att	Yds	Avg	LG	TD
Pruitt, M.	18	76	4.2	19	0
Pruitt, G.	5	26	5.2	15	0
White	2	7	3.5	6	0
Sipe	1	−3	−3.0	−3	0
TOTAL	26	106	4.1	19	0

Passing	Att	Cp	Yds	TD	LG	Int	Tk/Yds
Sipe	33	16	180	1	39	1	2/19
TOTAL	33	16	180	1	39	1	2/19

Receiving	No	Yds	LG	TD
Pruitt, G.	4	33	11	0
Rucker	3	77	38	1
Newsome	3	36	39	0
Pruitt, M.	3	11	6	0
White	2	12	8	0
Feacher	1	11	11	0
TOTAL	16	180	39	1

Interceptions	No	Yds	Avg	LG	TD
Ambrose	1	0	0.0	0	0
Flint	1	33	33.0	33	0
TOTAL	2	33	16.5	33	0

Punting	No	Yds	Avg	TB	In 20	LP
Cox	5	212	42.4	0	1	66
TOTAL	5	212	42.4	0	1	66

Punt Returns	No	FC	Yds	Avg	LG	TD
Hall	0		50	16.7	40	0
TOTAL	0		50	16.7	40	0

Kickoff Rets	No	Yds	Avg	LG	TD
Hall	3	82	27.3	33	0
TOTAL	3	82	27.3	33	0

Fumbles	No	Own Rec	Yds	TD	Opp Rec	Yds	TD	OB
Hall	1	0	0	0	0	0	0	0
TOTAL	1	0	0	0	0	0	0	0

SAN FRANCISCO 49ERS

Rushing	Att	Yds	Avg	LG	TD
Easley	16	59	3.7	9	0
Hofer	10	33	3.3	6	0
Patton	4	15	3.8	9	0
Davis	2	6	3.0	3	0
Montana	2	5	2.5	5	0
Solomon	1	0	0.0	9	0
TOTAL	35	118	3.4	9	0

Passing	Att	Cp	Yds	TD	LG	Int	Tk/Yds
Montana	42	24	213	0	18	2	3/26
TOTAL	42	24	213	0	18	2	3/26

Receiving	No	Yds	LG	TD
Hofer	7	64	16	0
Clark	6	52	15	0
Solomon	3	35	18	0
Cooper	3	21	9	0
Young	2	16	12	0
Patton	1	11	11	0
Shumann	1	8	8	0
Easley	1	6	6	0
TOTAL	24	213	18	0

Interceptions	No	Yds	Avg	LG	TD
Hicks	1	10	10.0	10	0
TOTAL	1	10	10.0	10	0

Punting	No	Yds	Avg	TB	In 20	LP
Miller	4	144	36.0	1	0	43
TOTAL	4	144	36.0	1	0	43

Punt Returns	No	FC	Yds	Avg	LG	TD
Solomon	2	0	22	11.0	15	0
TOTAL	2	0	22	11.0	15	0

Kickoff Rets	No	Yds	Avg	LG	TD
Lawrence	2	52	26.0	29	0
TOTAL	2	52	26.0	29	0

Fumbles	No	Own Rec	Own Yds	Own TD	Opp Rec	Opp Yds	Opp TD	OB
Shumann	1	0	0	0	0	0	0	1
Ring	0	0	0	0	1	0	0	0
TOTAL	1	0	0	0	1	0	0	1

GAME SUMMARY

Visitor: San Francisco 49ers **vs.** **Home:** Los Angeles Rams
Date: 22 November 1981   **At:** Anaheim Stadium
Day of Week: Sunday   **Starting Time:** 1:02 P.M.
Weather: Hazy sunshine
Temperature: 68°F   **Wind and Direction:** SW 5 mph
ATTENDANCE:
Tickets Distributed: 69,006   **Actual:** 63,456   **Time:** 3:15

SCORING BY QUARTER

	1	2	3	4	OT	TOTAL
San Francisco 49ers	3	7	17	6		33
LA Rams	0	17	7	7		31

SCORING BY PLAY AND DRIVE

Team	Per.	Elapsed Time	Scoring Play	Vis.	Home
SF	1	7:27	FG Wersching 47 yards (11–62)	3	0
LA	2	1:03	FG Corral 44 yards (13–53)	3	3
LA	2	9:00	Tyler 22 pass from Pastorini (Corral kick) (11–80)	3	10
SF	2	11:13	Davis 1 run (Wersching kick) (5–74)	10	10
LA	2	14:37	Dennard 7 pass from Guman (Corral kick) (13–80)	10	17
SF	3	0:18	Lawrence 92 kickoff return (Wersching kick)	17	17
SF	3	6:36	FG Wersching 34 yards (8–52)	20	17
SF	3	9:27	Lott 25 inter. return (Wersching kick)	27	17
LA	3	12:56	Arnold 2 pass from Haden (Corral kick) (9–80)	27	24
SF	4	4:50	FG Wersching 32 yards (7–45)	30	24
LA	4	13:09	Tyler 1 run (Corral kick) (15–90)	30	31
SF	4	15:00	FG Wersching 37 yards (13–61)	33	31

FINAL TEAM STATISTICS

	49ERS	RAMS
Total first downs	19	27
By rushing	4	15
By passing	12	10
By penalty	3	2
Third down efficiency	6/13–46.2%	10/17–58.8%
Total net yards	330	411
Total offensive plays*	61	80
Average gain per offensive play	5.4	5.1
Net yards rushing	71	203
Total rushing plays	28	47
Average gain per rushing play	2.5	4.3
Net yards passing	259	208
Times thrown/yds. lost att. to pass	3/24	1/0
Gross yards passing	283	208
Pass atts./completions/had intercepted	30/19/1	32/18/1
Avg. gain per pass play*	7.9	6.3
Punts—number/average	2/44.0	4/44.8
Had blocked	0	0
Total return yardage	220	91
Number/yards punt returns	2/12	1/5
Number/yards kickoff returns	5/183	5/86
Number/yards interception returns	1/25	1/0
Penalties—number/yards	5/51	7/71
Fumbles—number/lost	1/1	4/1
Touchdowns	3	4
Rushing	1	1
Passing	0	3
Returns	2	0
Extra points made/attempts	3/3	4/4
Field goals made/attempts	4/4	1/1
Time of possession	25:00	35:00

*Includes times thrown passing

INDIVIDUAL TEAM STATISTICS

San Francisco 49ers

Rushing	Att	Yds	Avg	LG	TD
Patton	8	20	2.5	6	0
Davis	8	23	2.9	14	1
Cooper	4	4	1.0	4	0
Montana	1	−1	−1.0	−1	0
Hofer	5	16	3.2	4	0
Lawrence	2	9	4.5	7	0
TOTAL	28	71	2.5	14	1

Passing	Att	Cp	Yds	TD	LG	Int	Tk/Yds
Montana	30	19	283	0	44	1	3/24
TOTAL	30	19	283	0	44	1	3/24

Receiving	No	Yds	LG	TD
Shumann	1	7	7	0
Young	2	18	14	0
Solomon	5	124	44	0
Cooper	5	55	24	0
Clark	4	59	23	0
Hofer	2	20	12	0
TOTAL	19	283	44	0

Interceptions	No	Yds	Avg	LG	TD
Lott	1	25		25	1
TOTAL	1	25		25	1

Punting	No	Yds	Avg	TB	In 20	LP
Miller	2	88	44.0	1	0	55
TOTAL	2	88	44.0	1	0	55

Punt Returns	No	FC	Yds	Avg	LG	TD
Hicks	2	0	12		7	0
Solomon	0	1	0		0	0
TOTAL	2	1	12		7	0

Kickoff Rets	No	Yds	Avg	LG	TD
Lawrence	3	138		92	1
Ring	2	45		24	0
TOTAL	5	183		92	1

Fumbles	No	Own Rec	Yds	TD	Opp Rec	Yds	TD	OB
Turner	0	0	0	0	1	0	0	0
Hofer	1	0	0	0	0	0	0	0
TOTAL	1	0	0	0	1	0	0	0

Los Angeles Rams

Rushing	Att	Yds	Avg	LG	TD
Tyler	23	97	4.2	13	1
Guman	17	64	3.8	12	0
Pastorini	2	13	6.5	13	0
Dennard	1	14	14.0	14	0
Bryant	2	4	2.0	4	0
Thomas, J.	1	2	2.0	2	0
Haden	1	9	9.0	9	0
TOTAL	47	203	4.3	14	1

Passing	Att	Cp	Yds	TD	LG	Int	Tk/Yds
Pastorini	18	8	79	1	22	1	0/0
Guman	1	1	7	1	7	0	0/0
Haden	13	9	122	1	43	0	1/0
TOTAL	32	18	208	3	43	1	1/0

Receiving	No	Yds	LG	TD
Tyler	4	39	22	1
Dennard	5	56	22	1
Thomas, J.	1	5	5	0
Guman	3	28	14	0
Arnold	2	22	20	1
Bryant	1	7	7	0
Waddy	1	8	8	0
Hill, D.	1	43	43	0
TOTAL	18	208	43	3

Interceptions	No	Yds	Avg	LG	TD
Cromwell	1	0		0	0
TOTAL	1	0		0	0

Punting	No	Yds	Avg	TB	In 20	LP
Corral	4	179	44.8	0	1	50
TOTAL	4	179	44.8	0	1	50

Punt Returns	No	FC	Yds	Avg	LG	TD
Irvin	1	0	5		5	0
TOTAL	1	0	5		5	0

Kickoff Rets	No	Yds	Avg	LG	TD
Hill, D.	5	86		29	0
TOTAL	5	86		29	0

| | | Own | | | | Opp | | |
Fumbles	No	Rec	Yds	TD	Rec	Yds	TD	OB
Pastorini	1	0	0	0	0	0	0	0
Gyman	1	0	0	0	0	0	0	1
Tyler	1	1	0	0	0	0	0	0
Harris	0	0	0	0	1	0	0	0
Hill, D.	1	1	0	0	0	0	0	0
TOTAL	4	2	0	0	1	0	0	1

GAME SUMMARY

Visitor: New York Giants   vs.   **Home:** San Francisco 49ers
Date: 29 November 1981   **At:** Candlestick Park, SF
Day of Week: Sunday   **Starting Time:** 1:01 P.M.
Weather: Clearing at kickoff
Temperature: 59°F   **Wind and Direction:** SW 5–7 mph
ATTENDANCE:
Tickets Distributed: 61,081   **Actual:** 57,186   **Time:** 3:09

SCORING BY QUARTER

	1	2	3	4	OT	TOTAL
New York Giants	0	3	0	7		10
San Francisco 49ers	7	7	0	3		17

SCORING BY PLAY AND DRIVE

Team	Per.	Elapsed Time	Scoring Play	Score Vis.	Home
SF	1	10:13	Davis 1 run (Wersching kick)—16 yards, 7 plays	0	7
SF	2	2:56	Montana 20 run (Wersching kick)—40 yards, 6 plays	0	14
NY	2	13:36	Danelo FG 52—5 yards, 4 plays	3	14
NY	4	0:06	Carpenter 3 run (Danelo kick)—76 yards, 11 plays	10	14
SF	4	7:43	Wersching FG 23—72 yards, 16 plays	10	17

FINAL TEAM STATISTICS

	GIANTS	49ERS
Total first downs	12	19
By rushing	5	5
By passing	6	14
By penalty	1	0
Third down efficiency	5/16–31.3%	11/25–44.0%
Total net yards	223	337
Total offensive plays*	58	82
Average gain per offensive play	3.8	4.1
Net yards rushing	80	123
Total rushing plays	22	39
Average gain per rushing play	3.6	3.2
Net yards passing	143	214
Times thrown/yds. lost att. to pass	2/19	3/20
Gross yards passing	162	234
Pass atts./completions/had intercepted	34/13/3	40/27/0
Avg. gain per pass play*	4.0	5.0
Punts—number/average	6/42.8	8/37.5
Had blocked	0	0
Total return yardage	119	136
Number/yards punt returns	6/33	4/27
Number/yards kickoff returns	4/86	2/48
Number/yards interception returns	0/0	3/61
Penalties—number/yards	9/65	5/48
Fumbles—number/lost	3/2	1/0
Touchdowns	1	2
Rushing	1	2
Passing	0	0
Returns	0	0
Extra points made/attempts	1/1	2/2
Field goals made/attempts	1/1	1/3
Time of possession	21:44	38:16

*Includes times thrown passing

INDIVIDUAL TEAM STATISTICS

New York Giants

Rushing	Att	Yds	Avg	LG	TD
Brunner	1	−1	−1.0	−1	0
Carpenter	13	40	3.1	13	1
Forte	7	31	4.4	12	0
Perkins	1	10	10.0	10	0
TOTAL	22	80	3.6	13	1

Passing	Att	Cp	Yds	TD	LG	Int	Tk/Yds
Brunner	34	13	162	0	29	3	2/19
TOTAL	34	13	162	0	29	3	2/19

Receiving	No	Yds	LG	TD
Carpenter	5	55	23	0
Forte	1	5	5	0
Friede	2	21	13	0
Gray	2	40	29	0
Mullady	1	13	13	0
Perkins	2	28	15	0
TOTAL	13	162	29	0

Interceptions	No	Yds	Avg	LG	TD
TOTAL	0	0	0.0	0	0

Punting	No	Yds	Avg	TB	In 20	LP
Jennings	6	257	42.8	0	1	51
TOTAL	6	257	42.8	0	1	51

Punt Returns	No	FC	Yds	Avg	LG	TD
Bright	5	0	32	6.4	16	0
Jackson, T.	1	0	1	1.0	1	0
Pitman	0	1	0	0.0	0	0
TOTAL	6	1	33	5.5	16	0

Kickoff Rets	No	Yds	Avg	LG	TD
Pitman	2	45	22.5	23	0
Dennis	1	17	17.0	17	0
Reece	1	24	24.0	24	0
TOTAL	4	86	21.5	24	0

Fumbles	No	Own Rec	Yds	TD	Opp Rec	Yds	TD	OB
Carpenter	1	0	0	0	0	0	0	0
Perkins	1	0	0	0	0	0	0	0
Pitman	1	1	0	0	0	0	0	0
TOTAL	3	1	0	0	0	0	0	0

San Francisco 49ers

Rushing	Att	Yds	Avg	LG	TD
Clark	1	5	5.0	5	0
Cooper	3	12	4.0	6	0
Davis	11	21	1.9	4	1
Lawrence	2	−7	−3.5	−3	0
Hofer	8	33	4.1	9	0
Montana	2	24	12.0	20	1
Patton	7	20	2.9	5	0
Ring	4	9	2.3	5	0
Solomon	1	6	6.0	6	0
TOTAL	39	123	3.1	20	2

Passing	Att	Cp	Yds	TD	LG	Int	Tk/Yds
Montana	39	27	234	0	26	0	3/20
Clark	1	0	0	0	0	0	0/0
TOTAL	40	27	234	0	26	0	3/20

Receiving	No	Yds	LG	TD
Clark	7	87	16	0
Cooper	4	37	26	0
Davis	2	−4	−2	0
Hofer	4	31	17	0
Lawrence	1	2	2	0
Patton	5	23	9	0
Solomon	1	25	25	0
Young	3	33	13	0
TOTAL	27	234	26	0

Interceptions	No	Yds	Avg	LG	TD
Hicks	1	54	54.0	54	0
Williamson	2	7	3.5	7	0
TOTAL	3	61	20.3	54	0

Punting	No	Yds	Avg	TB	In 20	LP
Miller	8	300	37.5	1	0	51
TOTAL	8	300	37.5	1	0	51

Punt Returns	No	FC	Yds	Avg	LG	TD
Hicks	3	0	19	6.3	14	0
Solomon	1	0	8	8.0	8	0
TOTAL	4	0	27	6.8	14	0

Kickoff Rets	No	Yds	Avg	LG	TD
Lawrence	1	25	25.0	25	0
Ring	1	23	23.0	23	0
TOTAL	2	48	24.0	25	0

Fumbles	No	Own Rec	Yds	TD	Opp Rec	Yds	TD	OB
Patton	1	0	0	0	0	0	0	0
Fahnhorst	0	1	0	0	0	0	0	0
Turner	0	0	0	0	1	0	0	0
Williamson	0	0	0	0	1	3	0	0
TOTAL	1	1	0	0	2	3	0	0

GAME SUMMARY

Visitor: San Francisco 49ers   **vs.**   **Home:** Cincinnati Bengals
Date: 5 December 1981   **At:** Riverfront Stadium
Day of Week: Sunday   **Starting Time:** 1:00 P.M.
Weather: Sunny
Temperature: 34°F   **Wind and Direction:** SW 9 mph
ATTENDANCE:
Tickets Distributed: 59,441   **Actual:** 56,796   **Time:** 3:05

SCORING BY QUARTER

	1	2	3	4	OT	TOTAL
San Francisco 49ers	7	7	0	7		21
Cincinnati Bengals	0	3	0	0		3

SCORING BY PLAY AND DRIVE

Team	Per.	Elapsed Time	Scoring Play	Score Vis.	Home
SF	1	7:59	Ring 4 pass from Montana (Wersching kick) (15–66)	7	0
CIN	2	12:28	FG Breech 30 (11–61)	7	3
SF	2	14:58	Clark 15 pass from Montana (Wersching kick) (10–80)	10	3
SF	4	8:32	Montana 1 run (Wersching kick) (8–40)	21	3

[208]

FINAL TEAM STATISTICS

	49ERS	BENGALS
Total first downs	24	24
By rushing	11	11
By passing	11	12
By penalty	2	1
Third down efficiency	8/16–50%	4/9–44%
Total net yards	325	345
Total offensive plays*	72	61
Average gain per offensive play	4.5	5.7
Net yards rushing	146	155
Total rushing plays	35	20
Average gain per rushing play	4.2	7.8
Net yards passing	190	199
Times thrown/yds. lost att. to pass	1/8	3/21
Gross yards passing	187	211
Pass atts./completions/had intercepted	37/23/1	37/20/2
Avg. gain per pass play*	4.8	4.6
Punts—number/average	6/36.8	3/45.6
Had blocked	0	0
Total return yardage	40	102
Number/yards punt returns	1/10	2/12
Number/yards kickoff returns	1/17	4/90
Number/yards interception returns	3/13	1/0
Penalties—number/yards	7/55	9/70
Fumbles—number/lost	0/0	4/3
Touchdowns	3	0
Rushing	1	0
Passing	2	0
Returns	0	0
Extra points made/attempts	3/3	0/0
Field goals made/attempts	0/0	1/1
Time of possession	26:48	33:12

*Includes times thrown passing

INDIVIDUAL TEAM STATISTICS

Cincinnati Bengals

Rushing	Att	Yds	Avg	LG	TD
Alexander	4	24	6.0	16	0
Johnson	12	86	7.2	17	0
Anderson	4	45	11.3	19	0
TOTAL	20	155	7.8	19	0

Passing	Att	Cp	Yds	TD	LG	Int	Tk/Yds
Anderson	20	11	97	0	19	2	1/2
Thompson	18	10	114	0	20	1	2/19
TOTAL	28	21	211	0	20	3	3/21

Receiving	No	Yds	LG	TD
Ross	7	69	11	0
Collinsworth	3	32	19	0
Curtis	1	10	10	0
Johnson	4	27	13	0
Alexander	1	6	6	0
Kreider	4	57	20	0
Harris	1	11	11	0
TOTAL	21	211	20	0

Interceptions	No	Yds	Avg	LG	TD
Riley	1	0		0	0
TOTAL	1	0		0	0

Punting	No	Yds	Avg	TB	In 20	LP
McInally	3	137	45.6	1	1	51
TOTAL	3	137	45.6	1	1	51

Punt Returns	No	FC	Yds	Avg	LG	TD
Fuller	2	1	12		10	0
TOTAL	2	1	12		10	0

Kickoff Rets	No	Yds	Avg	LG	TD
Verser	3	90		39	0
Kemp	1	0		0	0
TOTAL	4	90		39	0

Fumbles	No	Own Rec	Yds	TD	Opp Rec	Yds	TD	OB
Johnson	1	0	0	0	0	0	0	0
Collinsworth	1	0	0	0	0	0	0	1
Ross	1	0	0	0	0	0	0	0
Kreider	1	0	0	0	0	0	0	0
TOTAL	4	0	0	0	0	0	0	1

San Francisco 49ers

Rushing	Att	Yds	Avg	LG	TD
Cooper	12	62	5.2	18	0
Patton	10	36	3.6	14	0
Davis	8	21	2.6	8	0
Lawrence	1	5	5.0	5	0
Ring	2	8	4.0	9	0
Montana	2	14	7.0	13	1
TOTAL	35	146	4.2	18	1

Passing	Att	Cp	Yds	TD	LG	Int	Tk/Yds
Montana	34	23	187	2	20	1	1/8
TOTAL	34	23	187	2	20	1	1/8

Receiving	No	Yds	LG	TD
Young	3	22	9	0
Shumann	1	6	6	0
Clark	6	78	20	1
Ring	1	4	4	1
Cooper	6	34	18	0
Wilson	2	28	16	0
Patton	3	11	6	0
Ramson	1	4	4	0
TOTAL	23	187	20	2

Interceptions	No	Yds	Avg	LG	TD
Lott	1	13		13	0
Turner	1	2		0	0
Wright	1	0		0	0
TOTAL	3	13		13	0

Punting	No	Yds	Avg	TB	In 20	LP
Miller	6	221	36.8	2	1	47
TOTAL	6	221	36.8	2	1	47

Punt Returns	No	FC	Yds	Avg	LG	TD
Hicks	1	0	10		10	0
TOTAL	1	0	10		10	0

Kickoff Rets	No	Yds	Avg	LG	TD
Ring	1	17		17	0
TOTAL	1	17		17	0

Fumbles	No	Own Rec	Yds	TD	Opp Rec	Yds	TD	OB
Leopold	0	0	0	0	1	0	0	0
Hicks	0	0	0	0	2	0	0	0
TOTAL	0	0	0	0	3	0	0	0

GAME SUMMARY

Visitor: Houston Oilers   **vs.**   **Home:** San Francisco 49ers
Date: 13 December 1981   **At:** Candlestick Park, SF
Day of Week: Sunday   **Starting Time:** 1:01 P.M.
Weather: Overcast, light rain
Temperature: 63°F   **Wind and Direction:** negligible
ATTENDANCE:
Tickets Distributed: 61,119   **Actual:** 55,707   **Time:** 2:55

SCORING BY QUARTER

	1	2	3	4	OT	TOTAL
Houston Oilers	0	0	0	6		6
San Francisco 49ers	0	0	21	7		28

SCORING BY PLAY AND DRIVE

Team	Per.	Elapsed Time	Scoring Play	Vis.	Home
SF	3	6:04	Patton 3 run (Wersching kick) 69 yards, 10 plays	0	7
SF	3	11:13	Cooper 3 run (Wersching kick) 65 yards, 9 plays	0	14
SF	3	13:26	Clark 2 pass from Montana (Wersching kick) 26 yards, 4 plays	0	21
SF	4	5:45	Wilson 27 pass from Benjamin (Wersching kick) 76 yards, 10 plays	0	28
HOU	4	14:13	Campbell 1 run (Fritsch kick) blocked (Board) 59 yards, 8 plays	7	28

FINAL TEAM STATISTICS

	OILERS	49ERS
Total first downs	11	22
By rushing	5	7
By passing	4	14
By penalty	2	1
Third down efficiency	4/14–28.6%	6/14–42.9%
Total net yards	186	414
Total offensive plays*	53	67
Average gain per offensive play	3.5	6.2
Net yards rushing	56	148
Total rushing plays	22	29
Average gain per rushing play	2.5	5.1
Net yards passing	130	266
Times thrown/yds. lost att. to pass	1/10	3/20
Gross yards passing	140	286
Pass atts./completions/had intercepted	30/21/0	35/25/0
Avg. gain per pass play*	4.2	7.0
Punts—number/average	7/36.4	6/42.3
Had blocked	0	0
Total return yardage	163	34
Number/yards punt returns	5/61	5/16
Number/yards kickoff returns	5/102	1/18
Number/yards interception returns	0/0	0/0
Penalties—number/yards	8/47	8/77
Fumbles—number/lost	2/2	3/0
Touchdowns	0	4
Rushing	0	2
Passing	0	2
Returns	0	0
Extra points made/attempts	1/0	4/4
Field goals made/attempts	0/0	0/0
Time of possession	27:40	32:20

*Includes times thrown passing

INDIVIDUAL TEAM STATISTICS

Houston Oilers

Rushing	Att	Yds	Avg	LG	TD
Campbell	18	45	2.5	7	1
Armstrong	3	11	3.7	7	0
Nielsen	1	0	0.0	0	0
TOTAL	22	56	2.5	7	1

Passing	Att	Cp	Yds	TD	LG	Int	Tk/Yds
Nielsen	30	21	140	0	25	0	1/10
TOTAL	30	21	140	0	25	0	1/10

Receiving	No	Yds	LG	TD
Armstrong	9	62	25	0
Burrough	4	14	7	0
Casper	3	44	20	0
Coleman	2	11	7	0
Holston	2	7	4	0
Campbell	1	2	2	0
TOTAL	21	140	25	0

Interceptions	No	Yds	Avg	LG	TD
TOTAL	0	0	0.0	0	.0

Punting	No	Yds	Avg	TB	In 20	LP
Parsley	7	255	36.4	0	2	45
TOTAL	7	255	36.4	0	2	45

Punt Returns	No	FC	Yds	Avg	LG	TD
Roaches	5	0	61	12.2	40	0
TOTAL	5	0	61	12.2	40	0

Kickoff Rets	No	Yds	Avg	LG	TD
Riley	1	51	51.0	51	0
Roaches	2	32	16.0	17	0
Tullis	1	17	17.0	17	0
Hunt	1	2	2.0	2	0
TOTAL	5	102	20.4	51	0

Fumbles	No	Own Rec	Own Yds	Own TD	Opp Rec	Opp Yds	Opp TD	OB
Armstrong	1	0	0	0	0	0	0	0
Nielsen	1	0	0	0	0	0	0	0
TOTAL	2	0	0	0	0	0	0	0

San Francisco 49ers

Rushing	Att	Yds	Avg	LG	TD
Patton	9	57	6.3	28	1
Cooper	7	38	5.4	21	1
Ring	5	18	3.6	9	0
Clark	1	18	18.0	18	0
Davis	5	15	3.0	7	0
Montana	2	2	1.0	2	0
TOTAL	29	148	5.1	28	2

Passing	Att	Cp	Yds	TD	LG	Int	Tk/Yds
Montana	26	18	204	1	41	0	1/4
Benjamin	9	7	82	1	27	0	2/16
TOTAL	35	25	286	2	41	0	3/20

Receiving	No	Yds	LG	TD
Cooper	6	77	41	0
Clark	5	35	12	1
Young	4	36	16	0
Solomon	3	56	34	0
Wilson	2	36	27	1
Ring	2	24	21	0
Ramson	1	14	14	0
Hofer	1	11	11	0
Patton	1	−3	−3	0
TOTAL	25	286	41	2

Interceptions	No	Yds	Avg	LG	TD
TOTAL	0	0	0.0	0	0

Punting	No	Yds	Avg	TB	In 20	LP
Miller	6	254	42.3	1	1	65
TOTAL	6	254	42.3	1	1	65

Punt Returns	No	FC	Yds	Avg	LG	TD
Hicks	3	0	14	4.7	9	0
Solomon	2	1	2	1.0	2	0
TOTAL	5	1	16	3.2	9	0

Kickoff Rets	No	Yds	Avg	LG	TD
Ring	1	18	18.0	18	0
TOTAL	1	18	18.0	18	0

Fumbles	No	Own Rec	Yds	TD	Opp Rec	Yds	TD	OB
Montana	1	0	0	0	0	0	0	0
Patton	1	0	0	0	0	0	0	0
Solomon	1	0	0	0	0	0	0	1
Audick	0	2	0	0	0	0	0	0
Puki	0	0	0	0	1	0	0	0
Leopold	0	0	0	0	1	0	0	0
TOTAL	3	2	0	0	2	0	0	1

GAME SUMMARY

Visitor: San Francisco 49ers   **vs.**   **Home:** New Orleans Saints
Date: 20 December 1981   **At:** Louisiana Superdome
Day of Week: Sunday   **Starting Time:** 1:01 P.M.
Weather: Indoors
Temperature: 70°F   **Wind and Direction:** None
ATTENDANCE:
Tickets Distributed: 52,287   **Actual:** 43,639   **Time:** 2:41

SCORING BY QUARTER

	1	2	3	4	OT	TOTAL
San Francisco 49ers	7	7	0	7		21
New Orleans Saints	14	0	3	0		17

SCORING BY PLAY AND DRIVE

Team	Per.	Elapsed Time	Scoring Play	Score Vis.	Home
SF	1	6:33	Young 13 pass from Montana (Wersching kick) 10/72	7	0
NO	1	13:01	G. Rogers 6 run (Ricardo kick) 4/18	7	7
NO	1	14:47	G. Rogers 5 run (Ricardo kick) 3/7	7	14
SF	2	3:54	Solomon 2 pass from Montana (Wersching kick) 9/69	14	14
NO	3	12:25	FG Ricardo 27 10/26	14	17
SF	4	7:47	Davis 3 run (Wersching kick) 7/79	21	17

FINAL TEAM STATISTICS

	49ERS	SAINTS
Total first downs	19	15
By rushing	9	9
By passing	10	5
By penalty	0	1
Third down efficiency	8/13–62%	6/14–43%
Total net yards	349	222
Total offensive plays*	56	61
Average gain per offensive play	6.2	3.6
Net yards rushing	154	133
Total rushing plays	31	36
Average gain per rushing play	4.9	3.7
Net yards passing	195	89
Times thrown/yds. lost att. to pass	0/0	2/21
Gross yards passing	195	110
Pass atts./completions/had intercepted	25/17/1	23/14/1
Avg. gain per pass play*	7.8	4.4
Punts—number/average	4/46.0	4/34.8
Had blocked	0	0
Total return yardage	74	111
Number/yards punt returns	1/0	4/43
Number/yards kickoff returns	4/65	4/68
Number/yards interception returns	1/9	1/0
Penalties—number/yards	6/55	2/10
Fumbles—number/lost	3/2	1/0
Touchdowns	3	2
Rushing	1	2
Passing	2	0
Returns	0	0
Extra points made/attempts	3/3	2/2
Field goals made/attempts	0/0	1/1
Time of possession	26:03	33:57

*Includes times thrown passing

INDIVIDUAL TEAM STATISTICS

New Orleans Saints

Rushing	Att	Yds	Avg	LG	TD
Rogers, G.	30	107	3.6	9	2
Holmes	2	5	2.5	3	0
Rogers, J.	2	18	9.0	15	0
Tyler	2	3	1.5	2	0
TOTAL	36	133	3.7	15	2

Passing	Att	Cp	Yds	TD	LG	Int	Tk/Yds
Manning	21	14	110	0	20	1	2/21
Wilson, D.	2	0	0	0	0	0	0/0
TOTAL	23	14	110	0	21	1	2/21

Receiving	No	Yds	LG	TD
Holmes	1	8	8	0
Martini	1	7	7	0
Tyler	5	21	7	0
Merkens	1	12	12	0
Groth	1	10	10	0
Hardy	1	8	8	0
Thompson	2	21	13	0
Rogers, J.	1	3	3	0
Brenner	1	20	20	0
TOTAL	14	110	20	0

Interceptions	No	Yds	Avg	LG	TD
Wattelet	1	0		0	0
TOTAL	1	0		0	0

Punting	No	Yds	Avg	TB	In 20	LP
Erxleben	4	139	34.8	0	1	47
TOTAL	4	139	34.8	0	1	47

Punt Returns	No	FC	Yds	Avg	LG	TD
Groth	4	0	43		14	0
TOTAL	4	0	43		14	0

Kickoff Rets	No	Yds	Avg	LG	TD
Rogers, J.	1	23		23	0
Wilson, W.	2	39		24	0
Brock	1	6		6	0
TOTAL	4	68		24	0

Fumbles	No	Own Rec	Yds	TD	Opp Rec	Yds	TD	OB
Merkens	0	0	0	0	1	0	0	0
Pelluer	0	0	0	0	1	0	0	0
TOTAL	0	0	0	0	2	0	0	0

San Francisco 49ers

Rushing	Att	Yds	Avg	LG	TD
Patton	8	36	4.5	8	0
Cooper	1	−3	−3.0	0	0
Ring	11	71	6.5	16	0
Davis	6	19	3.1	4	1
Montana	1	10	10.0	10	0
Easley	2	4	2.0	3	0
Benjamin	1	1	1.0	1	0
Solomon	1	16	16.0	16	0
TOTAL	31	154	56.0	16	1

Passing	Att	Cp	Yds	TD	LG	Int	Tk/Yds
Montana	11	9	106	2	36	0	0/0
Benjamin	14	8	89	0	21	1	0/0
TOTAL	25	17	195	2	36	1	0/0

Receiving	No	Yds	LG	TD
Patton	4	25	11	0
Solomon	5	38	22	1
Young	1	13	13	1
Cooper	1	36	36	0
Easley	3	35	21	0
Clark	1	21	21	0
Ramson	2	27	16	0
TOTAL	17	195	36	2

Interceptions	No	Yds	Avg	LG	TD
Williamson	1	9		9	0
TOTAL	1	9		9	0

Punting	No	Yds	Avg	TB	In 20	LP
Miller	4	184	46.0	0	1	54
TOTAL	4	184	46.0	0	1	54

Punt Returns	No	FC	Yds	Avg	LG	TD
Solomon	1	0	0		0	0
Hicks	0	1	0		0	0
TOTAL	1	1	0		0	0

Kickoff Rets	No	Yds	Avg	LG	TD
Lawrence	2	24		22	0
Ring	2	41		22	0
TOTAL	4	65		22	0

Fumbles	No	Own Rec	Own Yds	TD	Opp Rec	Opp Yds	TD	OB
Solomon	1	0	0	0	0	0	0	0
Lawrence	1	0	0	0	0	0	0	0
Ring	1	0	0	0	0	0	0	1
TOTAL	3	0	0	0	0	0	0	1

GAME SUMMARY

Visitor: New York Giants **vs.** **Home:** San Francisco 49ers
Date: 3 January 1982 **At:** Candlestick Park, SF
Day of Week: Sunday **Starting Time:** 2:01 P.M.
Weather: Overcast, grey skies, with light rain at kickoff
Temperature: 45°F **Wind and Direction:** N 5–7 mph
ATTENDANCE:
Tickets Distributed: 60,994 **Actual:** 58,360 **Time:** 3:19

SCORING BY QUARTER

	1	2	3	4	OT	TOTAL
New York Giants	7	3	7	7		24
San Francisco 49ers	7	17	0	14		38

SCORING BY PLAY AND DRIVE

Team	Per.	Elapsed Time	Scoring Play	Score Vis.	Home
SF	1	5:57	Young 8 pass from Montana (Wersching kick)—85 yards, 13 plays	0	7
NY	1	12:15	Gray 72 pass from Brunner (Danelo kick)—72 yards, 2 plays	7	7
SF	2	0:03	Wersching FG 22—45 yards, 8 plays	7	10
SF	2	2:56	Solomon 58 pass from Montana (Wersching kick)—58 yards, 3 plays	7	17
SF	2	4:36	Patton 25 run (Wersching kick)—42 yards, 3 plays	7	24
NY	2	9:28	Danelo FG 48—51 yards, 11 plays	10	24
NY	3	3:47	Perkins 59 pass from Brunner (Danelo kick)—59 yards, 1 play	17	24
SF	4	4:23	Ring 3 run (Wersching kick)—36 yards, 6 plays	17	31
SF	4	11:49	Lott 20 interception return (Wersching kick)	17	38
NY	4	13:10	Perkins 17 pass from Brunner (Danelo kick)—62 yards, 7 plays	24	38

FINAL TEAM STATISTICS

	GIANTS	49ERS
Total first downs	13	24
By rushing	3	8
By passing	9	13
By penalty	1	3
Third down efficiency	6/16–37.5%	5/14–35.7%
Total net yards	346	423
Total offensive plays*	61	68
Average gain per offensive play	5.7	6.2
Net yards rushing	65	135
Total rushing plays	22	34
Average gain per rushing play	3.0	4.0
Net yards passing	281	288
Times thrown/yds. lost att. to pass	2/9	3/16
Gross yards passing	290	304
Pass atts./completions/had intercepted	37/16/2	31/20/1
Avg. gain per pass play*	7.2	8.5
Punts—number/average	4/43.8	5/41.2
Had blocked	0	0
Total return yardage	162	147
Number/yards punt returns	3/18	1/22
Number/yards kickoff returns	7/142	5/93
Number/yards interception returns	1/2	2/32
Penalties—number/yards	9/61	14/145
Fumbles—number/lost	4/2	2/0
Touchdowns	3	5
Rushing	0	2
Passing	3	2
Returns	0	1
Extra points made/attempts	3/3	5/5
Field goals made/attempts	1/2	1/2
Time of possession	25:42	34:18

*Includes times thrown passing

INDIVIDUAL TEAM STATISTICS

New York Giants

Rushing	Att	Yds	Avg	LG	TD
Carpenter	17	61	3.6	13	0
Bright	1	5	5.0	5	0
Perry	2	1	0.5	1	0
Brunner	2	−2	−1.0	0	0
TOTAL	22	65	3.0	13	0

Passing	Att	Cp	Yds	TD	LG	Int	Tk/Yds
Brunner	37	16	290	3	72	2	2/9
TOTAL	37	16	290	3	72	2	2/9

Receiving	No	Yds	LG	TD
Perkins	7	121	59	2
Gray	3	118	72	1
Carpenter	3	18	10	0
Young	2	15	10	0
Mistler	1	18	18	0
TOTAL	16	290	72	3

Interceptions	No	Yds	Avg	LG	TD
Currier	1	2	2.0	2	0
TOTAL	1	2	2.0	2	0

Punting	No	Yds	Avg	TB	In 20	LP
Jennings	4	175	43.8	0	0	51
TOTAL	4	175	43.8	0	0	51

Punt Returns	No	FC	Yds	Avg	LG	TD
Bright	3	0	18	6.0	12	0
TOTAL	3	0	18	6.0	12	0

Kickoff Rets	No	Yds	Avg	LG	TD
Bright	5	113	22.6	35	0
McLaughlin	1	15	15.0	15	0
Dennis	1	14	14.0	14	0
TOTAL	7	142	20.3	35	0

Fumbles	No	Own Rec	Own Yds	Own TD	Opp Rec	Opp Yds	Opp TD	OB
Brunner	2	1	0	0	0	0	0	0
Carpenter	1	0	0	0	0	0	0	0
Bright	1	0	0	0	0	0	0	0
Weston	0	1	0	0	0	0	0	0
TOTAL	4	2	0	0	0	0	0	0

San Francisco 49ers

Rushing	Att	Yds	Avg	LG	TD
Cooper	7	52	7.4	20	0
Patton	7	32	4.6	25	1
Ring	10	29	2.9	7	1
Solomon	1	12	12.0	12	0
Easley	4	9	2.3	5	0
Clark	1	6	6.0	6	0
Davis	1	4	4.0	4	0
Montana	3	−9	−3.0	2	0
TOTAL	34	135	4.0	25	2

Passing	Att	Cp	Yds	TD	LG	Int	Tk/Yds
Montana	31	20	304	2	58	1	3/16
TOTAL	31	20	304	2	58	1	3/16

Receiving	No	Yds	LG	TD
Solomon	6	107	58	1
Clark	5	104	39	0
Patton	2	38	28	0
Young	2	22	14	1
Wilson	2	21	15	0
Ramson	1	11	11	0
Elliott	1	5	5	0
Ring	1	−4	−4	0
TOTAL	20	304	58	2

Interceptions	No	Yds	Avg	LG	TD
Lott	2	32	16.0	20	1
TOTAL	2	32	16.0	20	1

Punting	No	Yds	Avg	TB	In 20	LP
Miller	5	206	41.2	0	2	52
TOTAL	5	206	41.2	0	2	52

Punt Returns	No	FC	Yds	Avg	LG	TD
Solomon	1	0	22	22.0	22	0
TOTAL	1	0	22	22.0	22	0

Kickoff Rets	No	Yds	Avg	LG	TD
Lawrence	3	88	29.3	47	0
Ring	1	5	5.0	5	0
Lott	1	0	0.0	0	0
TOTAL	5	93	18.6	47	0

Fumbles	No	Own Rec	Yds	TD	Opp Rec	Yds	TD	OB
Ring	1	1	0	0	0	0	0	0
Patton	1	1	0	0	0	0	0	0
Leopold	0	0	0	0	1	0	0	0
Turner	0	0	0	0	1	0	0	0
TOTAL	2	2	0	0	2	0	0	0

GAME SUMMARY

Visitor: Dallas Cowboys   **vs.**   **Home:** San Francisco 49ers
Date: 10 January 1982   **At:** Candlestick Park, SF
Day of Week: Sunday   **Starting Time:** 2:01 P.M.
Weather: Absolutely clear skies; light haze at horizon
Temperature: 45°F   **Wind and Direction:** Negligible
ATTENDANCE:
Tickets Distributed: 61,061   **Actual:** 60,525   **Time:** 3:13

SCORING BY QUARTER

	1	2	3	4	OT	TOTAL
Dallas Cowboys	10	7	0	10		27
San Francisco 49ers	7	7	7	7		28

SCORING BY PLAY AND DRIVE

Team	Per.	Elapsed Time	Scoring Play	Score Vis.	Home
SF	1	4:19	Solomon 8 pass from Montana (Wersching kick)—63 yards, 6 plays	0	7
DAL	1	10:16	Septien FG 44—44 yards, 9 plays	3	7
DAL	1	12:11	Hill 26 pass from D. White (Septien kick)—29 yards, 2 plays	10	7
SF	2	8:48	Clark 20 pass from Montana (Wersching kick)—47 yards, 4 plays	10	14
DAL	2	12:30	Dorsett 5 run (Septien kick)—80 yards, 8 plays	17	14
SF	3	9:16	Davis 2 run (Wersching kick)—13 yards, 4 plays	17	21
DAL	4	0:52	Septien FG 22—64 yards, 11 plays	20	21
DAL	4	4:19	Cosbie 21 pass from D. White (Septien kick)—50 yards, 4 plays	27	21
SF	4	14:09	Clark 6 pass from Montana (Wersching kick)—89 yards, 13 plays	27	28

FINAL TEAM STATISTICS

	COWBOYS	49ERS
Total first downs	16	26
By rushing	5	6
By passing	9	17
By penalty	2	3
Third down efficiency	5/13–38.5%	4/10–40.0%
Total net yards	250	393
Total offensive plays*	60	69
Average gain per offensive play	4.2	5.7
Net yards rushing	115	127
Total rushing plays	32	31
Average gain per rushing play	3.6	4.1
Net yards passing	135	266
Times thrown/yds. lost att. to pass	4/38	3/20
Gross yards passing	173	286
Pass atts./completions/had intercepted	24/16/1	35/22/3
Avg. gain per pass play*	4.8	7.0
Punts—number/average	6/39.3	3/35.7
Had blocked	0	0
Total return yardage	102	136
Number/yards punt returns	3/13	3/24
Number/yards kickoff returns	5/89	6/107
Number/yards interception returns	3/0	1/5
Penalties—number/yards	5/39	7/106
Fumbles—number/lost	4/2	3/3
Touchdowns	3	4
Rushing	1	1
Passing	2	3
Returns	0	0
Extra points made/attempts	3/3	4/4
Field goals made/attempts	2/2	0/0
Time of possession	32:57	27:03

*Includes times thrown passing

INDIVIDUAL TEAM STATISTICS

Dallas Cowboys

Rushing	Att	Yds	Avg	LG	TD
Dorsett	22	91	4.1	11	1
Jones, J.	4	14	3.5	7	0
Springs	5	10	2.0	3	0
White, D.	1	0	0.0	0	0
TOTAL	32	115	3.6	11	1

Passing	Att	Cp	Yds	TD	LG	Int	Tk/Yds
White, D.	24	16	173	2	31	1	4/38
TOTAL	24	16	173	2	31	1	4/38

Receiving	No	Yds	LG	TD
Jones, J.	3	17	10	0
DuPree	3	15	7	0
Springs	3	13	12	0
Hill	2	43	26	1
Pearson	1	31	31	0
Cosbie	1	21	21	1
Johnson	1	20	20	0
Saldi	1	9	9	0
Donley	1	4	4	0
TOTAL	16	173	31	2

Interceptions	No	Yds	Avg	LG	TD
Walls	2	0	0.0	0	0
White, R.	1	0	0.0	0	0
TOTAL	3	0	0.0	0	0

Punting	No	Yds	Avg	TB	In 20	LP
White, D.	6	236	39.3	1	1	49
TOTAL	6	236	39.3	1	1	49

Punt Returns	No	FC	Yds	Avg	LG	TD
Jones, J.	3	0	13	4.3	13	0
TOTAL	3	0	13	4.3	13	0

Kickoff Rets	No	Yds	Avg	LG	TD
Jones, J.	3	56	18.7	20	0
Newsome	2	33	16.5	19	0
TOTAL	5	89	17.8	20	0

Fumbles	No	Own Rec	Yds	TD	Opp Rec	Yds	TD	OB
Jones. J.	2	1	0	0	0	0	0	0
White, D.	2	1	0	0	0	0	0	0
Hegman	0	0	0	0	1	0	0	0
Bethea	0	0	0	0	1	0	0	0
Walls	0	0	0	0	1	0	0	0
TOTAL	4	2	0	0	3	0	0	0

San Francisco 49ers

Rushing	Att	Yds	Avg	LG	TD
Elliott	10	48	4.8	11	0
Cooper	8	35	4.4	11	0
Ring	6	27	4.5	11	0
Solomon	1	14	14.0	14	0
Easley	2	6	3.0	4	0
Davis	1	2	2.0	2	0
Montana	3	−5	−1.7	2	0
TOTAL	31	127	4.1	14	1

Passing	Att	Cp	Yds	TD	LG	Int	Tk/Yds
Montana	35	22	286	3	38	3	3/20
TOTAL	35	22	286	3	38	3	3/20

Receiving	No	Yds	LG	TD
Clark	8	120	38	2
Solomon	6	75	21	1
Young	4	45	17	0
Cooper	2	11	6	0
Elliott	1	24	24	0
Shumann	1	11	11	0
TOTAL	22	286	38	3

Interceptions	No	Yds	Avg	LG	TD
Leopold	1	5	5.0	5	0
TOTAL	1	5	5.0	5	0

Punting	No	Yds	Avg	TB	In 20	LP
Miller	3	107	35.7	0	0	37
TOTAL	3	107	35.7	0	0	37

Punt Returns	No	FC	Yds	Avg	LG	TD
Hicks	2	1	21	10.5	12	0
Solomon	1	1	3	3.0	3	0
TOTAL	3	2	24	8.0	12	0

Kickoff Rets	No	Yds	Avg	LG	TD
Lawrence	3	60	20.0	24	0
Ring	3	47	15.7	17	0
TOTAL	6	107	17.8	24	0

Fumbles	No	Own Rec	Yds	TD	Opp Rec	Yds	TD	OB
Ring	1	0	0	0	0	0	0	0
Montana	1	0	0	0	0	0	0	0
Easley	1	0	0	0	0	0	0	0
Lawrence	0	0	0	0	1	0	0	0
Stuckey	0	0	0	0	1	0	0	0
TOTAL	3	0	0	0	2	0	0	0

Chapter 13

Records and Statistics

49er club records set

INDIVIDUAL RECORDS	Former Record	Set or tied in 1981
Interceptions returned for touchdown, career	3, Rex Berry (1953-55)	3, Ronnie Lott (tied)
Interceptions returned for touchdown, season	1, many players	3, Lott
Interception return yards, season	159, Chuck Crist (1976)	239, Dwight Hicks
Interception return yards, game	94, Alvin Randolph (1966)	104, Hicks (vs. Wash.)
Longest fumble return	75, Clark Miller (1965)	80, Hicks (vs. Wash.)
Consecutive passes without an interception	95, John Brodie (1970)	122, Joe Montana
Consecutive games, at least one reception	28, Danny Abramowicz (1973-74)	31, Dwight Clark
Total yards punted, one season	3634, Tom Wittum (1976)	3858, Jim Miller
Extra-point percentage	100% by several players	100% Ray Wersching (30 of 30) tied

TEAM RECORDS	Former Record	Set or tied in 1981
Regular season home attendance	397,186 (1972)	435,182
Victories	10 (1970)	13
Consecutive victories	5 (several times)	7
Consecutive road victories	4 (1951-52)	6
Interceptions returned for touchdowns	3 (1966, 68, 72)	4
Offensive plays	1099 (1979)	1106
Pass completion percentage	62.6 percent (1957)	63.4 percent
Opponents' pass attempts	495 (1980)	514
Total yards punted	3634 (1976)	3858
Punts returned by opponents	52 (1976)	57
Punt return yards by opponents	587 (1963)	664

The Super Bowl roster

No.	Name	Pos.	Ht.	Wt.	Age	NFL Exp.	College
3	Jim Miller	P	5-11	183	24	2	Mississippi
7	Guy Benjamin	QB	6-3	210	26	4	Stanford
14	Ray Wersching	K	5-11	210	31	9	California
16	Joe Montana	QB	6-2	200	25	3	Notre Dame
20	Amos Lawrence	RB	5-10	179	23	R	N Carolina
21	Eric Wright	CB	6-1	180	22	R	Missouri
22	Dwight Hicks	S	6-1	189	25	3	Michigan
24	Rick Gervais	S	5-11	190	22	R	Stanford
27	Carlton Williamson	S	6-0	204	23	R	Pittsburgh
28	Lynn Thomas	CB	5-11	181	22	R	Pittsburgh
29	Saladin Martin	CB	6-1	180	25	2	San Diego St.
30	Bill Ring	RB	5-10	215	25	1	Brig. Young
31	Walt Easley	FB	6-1	226	24	R	West Virginia
32	Ricky Patton	RB	5-11	192	27	4	Jackson St.
35	Lenvil Elliott	RB	6-0	210	30	9	NE Missouri
38	Johnny Davis	RB	6-1	235	25	4	Alabama

No.	Name	Pos.	Ht.	Wt.	Age	NFL Exp.	College
42	Ronnie Lott	CB	6-0	199	22	R	USC
49	Earl Cooper	FB	6-2	227	24	2	Rice
51	Randy Cross	G	6-3	250	27	6	UCLA
52	Bobby Leopold	LB	6-1	215	24	2	Notre Dame
53	Milt McColl	LB	6-6	220	22	R	Stanford
54	Craig Puki	LB	6-1	231	24	2	Tennessee
56	Fred Quillan	C	6-5	260	25	4	Oregon
57	Dan Bunz	LB	6-4	225	26	4	Cal State—L.B.
58	Keena Turner	LB	6-2	219	23	2	Purdue
59	Willie Harper	LB	6-2	215	31	8	Nebraska
60	John Choma	G-C	6-6	261	26	1	Virginia
61	Dan Audick	T	6-3	253	27	4	Hawaii
62	Walt Downing	C-G	6-3	254	25	4	Michigan
64	Jack Reynolds	LB	6-1	232	34	12	Tennessee
65	Lawrence Pillers	DE	6-4	260	29	6	Alcorn A&M
66	Allan Kennedy	T	6-7	275	23	R	Wash. St.
68	John Ayers	G	6-5	260	28	5	W Texas St.
71	Keith Fahnhorst	T	6-6	263	29	8	Minnesota
74	Fred Dean	DE	6-2	230	29	7	Louisiana Tech
75	John Harty	DT	6-4	253	24	R	Iowa
76	Dwaine Board	DE	6-5	250	25	3	N Carolina A&T
78	Archie Reese	DT	6-3	262	25	4	Clemson
79	Jim Stuckey	DE	6-4	251	23	2	Clemson
80	Eason Ramson	TE	6-2	234	25	3	Wash. St.
84	Mike Shumann	WR	6-0	175	26	4	Florida St.
85	Mike Wilson	WR	6-3	210	23	R	Wash. St.
86	Charle Young	TE	6-4	234	30	9	USC
87	Dwight Clark	WR	6-4	210	24	3	Clemson
88	Freddie Solomon	WR	5-11	185	28	7	Tampa

Injured Reserve: Ken Bungarda, Ricky Churchman, Phil Francis, Eric Herring, Paul Hofer, Pete Kugler, Ed Judie, Gus Parham, George Visger.

Head Coach: Bill Walsh

Assistant Coaches: Cas Banaszek, Norb Hecker, Milt Jackson, Billie Matthews, Bobb McKittrick, Bill McPherson, Ray Rhodes, George Seifert, Chuck Studley, Al Vermeil, Sam Wyche.

AMERICAN FOOTBALL CONFERENCE

Eastern Division

	W	L	T	Pct.	Pts.	OP
•Miami	11	4	1	.719	345	275
♦NY Jets	10	5	1	.656	355	287
♦Buffalo	10	6	0	.625	311	276
Baltimore	2	14	0	.125	259	533
New England	2	14	0	.125	322	370

Central Division

	W	L	T	Pct.	Pts.	OP
•Cincinnati	12	4	0	.750	421	304
Pittsburgh	8	8	0	.500	356	297
Houston	7	9	0	.438	281	355
Cleveland	5	11	0	.313	276	375

Western Division

	W	L	T	Pct.	Pts.	OP
•San Diego	10	6	0	.625	478	390
Denver	10	6	0	.625	321	289
Kansas City	9	7	0	.563	343	290
Oakland	7	9	0	.438	273	343
Seattle	6	10	0	.375	322	388

AFC FIRST ROUND PLAYOFF
Buffalo 31, New York Jets 27

AFC DIVISIONAL PLAYOFF
Cincinnati 28, Buffalo 21
San Diego 41, Miami 38

AFC CHAMPIONSHIP
Cincinnati 27, San Diego 7

•Division Champion
♦Wild Card for Playoffs
NOTE: San Diego won AFC Western title over Denver on the basis of a better division record (6-2 to 5-3).

NATIONAL FOOTBALL CONFERENCE

Eastern Division

	W	L	T	Pct.	Pts.	OP
*Dallas	12	4	0	.750	367	277
♦Philadelphia	10	6	0	.625	368	221
♦NY Giants	9	7	0	.563	295	257
Washington	8	8	0	.500	347	349
St. Louis	7	9	0	.438	315	408

Central Division

	W	L	T	Pct.	Pts.	OP
*Tampa Bay	9	7	0	.563	315	268
Detroit	8	8	0	.500	397	322
Green Bay	8	8	0	.500	324	361
Minnesota	7	9	0	.438	325	369
Chicago	6	10	0	.375	253	324

Western Division

	W	L	T	Pct.	Pts.	OP
*San Francisco	13	3	0	.813	357	250
Atlanta	7	9	0	.438	426	355
Los Angeles	6	10	0	.375	303	351
New Orleans	4	12	0	.250	207	378

NFC FIRST ROUND PLAYOFF
New York Giants 27, Philadelphia 21

NFC DIVISIONAL PLAYOFF
SAN FRANCISCO 38, New York Giants 24
Dallas 38, Tampa Bay 0

NFC CHAMPIONSHIP
SAN FRANCISCO 28, Dallas 27

SUPER BOWL
SAN FRANCISCO 27, Cincinnati 21

*Division Champion
♦Wild Card for Playoffs

FINAL TEAM STATISTICS

	49ERS	Opp.
Time of Possession	8:27:28	7:33:30
Total First Downs	317	280
By rushing	110	113
By passing	183	144
By penalty	24	23
Third Down-Made/Att.	114/259	87/224
Third down efficiency	40.0%	38.8%
Total Net Yards	5484	4763
Avg. gain per game	342.8	297.7
Total offensive plays	1106	1014
Average gain per play	5.0	4.7
Net yards rushing	1941	1918
Avg. gain per game	121.3	119.9
Total rushing plays	560	464
Avg gain per rush	3.5	4.1
Net yards passing	3543	2845
Avg. net passing per game	221.4	177.8
Lost att. to pass	29/223	36/290
Gross yards passing	3766	3135
Attempts/completions	517/328	514/273
Percent complete	63.4	53.1
Had intercepted	13	27
Punts/Average	93/41.5	83/41.4
Net punting average	31.1	36.0
Punt Returns/Average	48/7.2	57/11.6
Kickoff Return/Average	45/20.2	67/20.7
Interceptions/Average Return	27/16.6	13/22.8
Penalties/Yards	92/752	108/866
Fumbles/Ball Lost	26/12	36/21
Touchdowns	43	30
By rushing	17	10
By passing	20	16
By returns	6	4
Extra points	42/43	29/30
Field goals	19/29	13/23
Safeties	0	1
Total Points	357	250
Avg. per Game	22.3	15.6

SCORE BY QUARTERS

	1	2	3	4	OT	Total
49ERS TOTAL	80	100	88	89	0	357
Opp. Total	40	76	55	79	0	250

Kickoff Rets	No	Yds	Avg	LG	TD
Lawrence	17	437	25.7	92T	1
Ring	10	217	21.7	29	0
Lott	7	111	15.9	20	0
Wilson	4	67	16.8	22	0
Jones	3	43	14.3	22	0
Hicks	1	22	22.0	22	0
Ramson	1	12	12.0	12	0
Patton	1	0	0.0	0	0
Davis	1	0	0.0	0	0
49ERS	45	909	20.2	92T	1
Opponents	67	1389	20.7	55	0

Punt Returns	No	FC	Yds	Avg	LG	TD
Solomon	29	6	173	6.0	19	0
Hicks	19	4	171	9.0	39	0
49ERS	48	10	344	7.2	39	0
Opponents	57	8	664	11.6	58T	1

Punting	No	Yds	Avg	TB	In 20	LG	Blk
Miller	93	3858	41.5	15	14	65	0
49ERS	93	3858	41.5	15	14	65	0
Opponents	83	3433	41.4	5	17	66	0

Field Goals	1–19	20–29	30–39	40–49	50+	Total
Wersching	2-2	7-7	4-7	4-7	0-0	17-23
Bahr	0-0	0-2	0-1	2-3	0-0	2-6
49ERS	2-2	7-9	4-8	6-10	0-0	19-29
Opponents	1-1	6-9	3-6	2-6	1-1	13-23

Wersching: (25*,32)(18*,40)(26*,32*)(42*,18*)(45*,37b)(48*)
(40,28*,29*,28*,28*)(47*,34*,32*,37*)(36b,40,23*)(-)(-)(-)
Bahr: (39,48)(47*,24b)(-)(43*,25)
*-Indicates Good; b-Indicates Blocked
Wersching missed games 2 through 5
Bahr played only in games 2 through 5

INDIVIDUAL STATISTICS

Rushing	Att	Yds	Avg	LG	TD
Patton	152	543	3.6	28	4
Cooper	98	330	3.4	23	1
Davis	94	297	3.2	14	7
Easley	76	224	2.9	9	1
Hofer	60	193	3.2	12	1
Ring	22	106	4.8	16	0
Montana	25	95	3.8	20	2
Lawrence	13	48	3.7	14	1
Solomon	9	43	4.8	16	0
Clark	3	32	10.7	18	0
Elliott	7	29	4.1	9	0
Benjamin	1	1	1.0	1	0
49ERS	560	1941	3.5	28	17
Opponents	464	1918	4.1	29	10

Receiving	No	Yds	Avg	LG	TD
Clark	85	1105	13.0	78T	4
Solomon	59	969	16.4	60T	8
Cooper	51	477	9.4	50	0
Young	37	400	10.8	29	5
Hofer	27	244	9.0	22	0
Patton	27	195	7.2	31T	1
Wilson	9	125	13.9	27T	1
Easley	9	62	6.9	21	0
Elliott	7	81	11.6	19	0
Ramson	4	45	11.3	16	0
Ring	3	28	9.3	21	1
Shumann	3	21	7.0	8	0
Lawrence	3	10	3.3	5	0
Davis	3	−1	−0.3	3	0
Peets	1	5	5.0	5	0
49ERS	328	3766	11.5	78T	20
Opponents	273	3135	11.5	67T	16

Interceptions	No	Yds	Avg	LG	TD
Hicks	9	239	26.6	72	1
Lott	7	117	16.7	41T	3
Williamson	4	44	11.0	28	0
Wright	3	26	8.7	26	0
McColl	1	22	22.0	22	0
Reynolds	1	0	0.0	0	0
Martin	1	0	0.0	0	0
Turner	1	0	0.0	0	0
49ERS	27	448	16.6	72	4
Opponents	13	297	22.8	101T	2

Scoring	TR	TP	TRT	FG	PAT	SF	TP
Wersching	0	0	0	17-23	30-30	0	81
Solomon	0	8	0	0-0	0-0	0	48
Davis	7	0	0	0-0	0-0	0	42
Patton	4	1	0	0-0	0-0	0	30
Young	0	5	0	0-0	0-0	0	30
Clark	0	4	0	0-0	0-0	0	24
Bahr	0	0	0	2-6	12-12	0	18
Lott	0	0	3	0-0	0-0	0	18
Hicks	0	0	2	0-0	0-0	0	12
Lawrence	1	0	1	0-0	0-0	0	12
Montana	2	0	0	0-0	0-0	0	12
Cooper	1	0	0	0-0	0-0	0	6
Easley	1	0	0	0-0	0-0	0	6
Hofer	1	0	0	0-0	0-0	0	6
Ring	0	1	0	0-0	0-0	0	6
Wilson	0	1	0	0-0	0-0	0	6
TEAM	0	0	0	0-0	0-1	0	0
49ERS	17	20	6	19-29	42-43	0	357
Opponents	10	16	4	13-23	29-30	1	250

Passing	Att	Comp	Yds	Pct	Avg/Att
Montana	488	311	3565	63.7	7.31
Benjamin	26	15	171	57.7	6.58
Easley	1	1	5	100.0	5.00
Solomon	1	1	25	100.0	25.00
Clark	1	0	0	0.0	0.00
49ERS	517	328	3766	63.4	7.28
Opponents	514	273	3135	53.1	6.10

Passing (cont)	TD	Pct TD	Int	Pct Int	LG	Lost/Att	Rating
Montana	19	3.9	12	2.5	78T	26/193	88.2
Benjamin	1	3.8	1	3.8	27	3/ 30	74.4
Easley	0	0.0	0	0.0	5	0/ 0	87.5
Solomon	0	0.0	0	0.0	25	0/ 0	118.8
Clark	0	0.0	0	0.0	0	0/ 0	0.0
49ERS	20	3.9	13	2.5	78T	29/223	87.8
Opponents	16	3.1	27	5.3	67	36/290	60.0

DEFENSIVE STATISTICS

Name	Tackles Total	Solo	Assists	Sacks
Jack Reynolds	117	66	51	0-0
Ronnie Lott	89	52	37	0-0
Keena Turner	84	58	26	3-25
Carlton Williamson	82	51	31	0-0
Dwight Hicks	76	60	16	0-0
Eric Wright	75	57	18	0-0
Willie Harper	72	43	29	1-4
Bobby Leopold	65	42	23	0.5-1
Dan Bunz	60	39	21	0-0
Lawrence Pillers	53	32	21	7-60
Archie Reese	53	36	17	0.5-4½
Dwaine Board	53	28	25	7-67½
Craig Puki	51	24	27	0-0
Jim Stuckey	48	33	16	2.5-6½
Fred Dean*	33	19	14	13-114¼
Lynn Thomas	26	16	10	0-0
Bill Ring	21	18	3	0-0
Milt McColl	19	13	6	1-9
Saladin Martin	18	14	4	0-0
Mike Wilson	12	5	7	0-0
John Harty	9	2	7	0.5-0
Rick Gervais	7	4	3	0-0
Amos Lawrence	5	3	2	0-0
Randy Cross	4	2	2	0-0
Eason Ramson	3	1	2	0-0
John Choma	2	2	0	0-0
John Ayers	1	1	0	0-0
Jim Miller	1	1	0	0-0
Earl Cooper	1	1	0	0-0
Freddie Solomon	1	1	0	0-0
Charle Young	1	1	0	0-0
Ricky Patton	1	1	0	0-0
Joe Montana	1	1	0	0-0
Dwight Clark	1	1	0	0-0
Dan Audick	1	0	1	0-0
Johnny Davis	1	0	1	0-0
Walt Easley	1	0	1	0-0
Others	29	19	10	0-0
49ERS' Totals**	1170	744	426	36-290
Opponents Totals	1251	845	406	29-223

| | Passes | | Fumbles | | Kicks |
Name	Int	Def	Rec	Forced	Blocked
Jack Reynolds	1-0	0	0	1	0
Ronnie Lott	7-117	22	2	4	0
Keena Turner	1-0	7	3	0	0
Carlton Williamson	3-44	19	2-3	1	0
Dwight Hicks	9-239	14	3-80	1	0
Eric Wright	3-26	24	2	1	0
Willie Harper	0-0	6	1	0	0
Bobby Leopold	0-0	5	2	0	0
Dan Bunz	0-0	0	2	1	0
Lawrence Pillers	0-0	4	0	0	0
Archie Reese	0-0	1	1	0	0
Dwaine Board	0-0	4	0	0	2±
Craig Puki	0-0	1	2	0	0
Jim Stuckey	0-0	5	1	0	0
Fred Dean	0-0	4	0	0	0
Lynn Thomas	0-0	3	0	0	0
Bill Ring	0-0	0	1	0	0
Milt McColl	1-22	1	0	0	0
Saladin Martin	1-0	10	1	0	0
Amos Lawrence	0-0	0	0	1	0
Others		0-0		0	1	0
49ERS' Totals**	27-448	129	21-83	11	2
Opponents Totals	13-297	79	12-76	9	3

*Fred Dean's totals include his three-game San Diego Chargers stats of 8 total tackles: 3 solo tackles, 5 assists, 1 sack for 8 yards, and 1 pass defensed.
**49ers' totals do not include Fred Dean's San Diego stats.

Chapter 14

History of the 49ers

How they got the name

From the beginning, in 1946, the San Francisco football team has been called the "Forty-Niners," spelled out.

The reference was specific and appropriate, to the people who had flooded into and shaped Northern California in the Gold Rush of 1849—less than 100 years before.

The force behind the new team in a new league was Tony Morabito, who was in the lumber business. He and two partners, Allen E. Sorrell and Ernest Turre, paid $25,000 for a franchise in the All-American Football Conference (which would start play in 1946), at a time when no major league team in any sport operated farther west than St. Louis.

Among the suggested names tossed around then were several adopted later by other teams in this area: Golden Gaters (of World Team Tennis), Pioneers (of the Women's Professional Basketball League) and Seals (of the National Hockey League).

But the partners decided on Forty-Niners for its connotation of risking greatly to gain gold.

The original symbol of a 49er (the present form of the name) was a picture of a prospector, wearing boots, checked pants, and a lumberjack shirt. His hair and mustache are windblown, his hat gone, and in each hand there is a six-shooter being fired. One shot just misses his foot, one just misses his head.

It was suggested the prospector depicted was drunk.

"He WAS drunk," Morabito is reported to have said years later. "In the original picture, which was featured on the side of railway freight cars, there was a saloon in the background."

The prospector has long since disappeared from official 49er literature. After the 49ers joined the National Football League in 1950, football marketing reached sophisticated levels and the painted helmet became the standard emblem for all teams.

Playoff history

Before 1981, the 49ers had only six playoff games in 31 seasons as a member of the National Football League. The 49ers also played two playoff games in 1949, the last of their four seasons in the All-American Football Conference, in which they began their existence.

In the AAFC, they had spent the first three years in the same division as the all-conquering Cleveland Browns, so they finished second every time, even when they were 12-2 in 1948. In 1949, the league was down to seven teams, playing a round-robin schedule without divisions, so there was a one-vs.-four and two-vs.-three first-round playoff.

Early in the season, the 49ers reached a peak their oldest fans still glory in: They crushed the Browns, 56-28, at Kezar. But that turned out to be the only game the Browns lost, while tying two others, so their 9-1-2 record left them in first place. The 49ers (who lost a rematch in Cleveland 30-28) placed second with 9-3 and had to play the Yankees, a combined New York-Brooklyn entry that had finished 8-4.

The 49ers won, 17-7, while Cleveland brushed by Buffalo, so the 49ers were finally in a championship showdown to be played in Cleveland.

But two days before the game, the AAFC went out of business with the announcement it was "merging" with the NFL—a merger that would include only the Browns, the 49ers and the Baltimore Colts (who soon faded out and were not related to the present Baltimore Colts).

So the final AAFC championship game didn't mean much to the public, and only 22,500 showed up in the 80,000-seat Municipal Stadium. The Browns won, 21-7, and collected $266.11 a man; the losing 49ers got $172.61.

As members of the NFL, the 49ers played one special playoff—in 1957 with Detroit to resolve a tie for first place in the division—and five "regular" playoff games in the pattern established in 1970 after another merger, the large one with the American Football League.

They lost the special playoff. In 1970 and 1971, they won first-round games after finishing first in their division, but lost the NFC championship game, each time to Dallas. In 1972, they lost to Dallas in the first round.

49ERS ALL-TIME STANDINGS
ALL-AMERICAN CONFERENCE

	W	L	T	Pct	Pts	Opp Pts	Div Stdg
1946	9	5	0	.643	307	189	2nd
1947	8	4	2	.667	327	264	2nd
1948	12	2	0	.857	495	248	2nd
1949	9	3	0	.750	416	227	2nd
TOTALS	38	14	2	.731	1545	928	

San Francisco lost championship playoff to Cleveland, 21-7

NATIONAL FOOTBALL LEAGUE

	W	L	T	Pct	Pts	Opp Pts	Div Stdg
1950	3	9	0	.250	213	300	Tied 5th
1951	7	4	1	.636	255	205	Tied 2nd
1952	7	5	0	.583	285	221	3rd
1953	9	3	0	.750	372	237	2nd
1954	7	4	1	.636	313	251	3rd
1955	4	8	0	.333	216	298	5th
1956	5	6	1	.455	233	284	3rd
1957	8	4	0	.667	260	264	*Tied 1st
1958	6	6	0	.500	257	324	4th
1959	7	5	0	.583	255	237	Tied 3rd
1960	7	5	0	.583	208	205	Tied 2nd
1961	7	6	1	.538	346	272	5th
1962	6	8	0	.428	282	331	5th
1963	2	12	0	.143	198	391	7th
1964	4	10	0	.285	236	330	7th
1965	7	6	1	.538	421	402	4th
1966	6	6	2	.500	320	325	4th
1967	7	7	0	.500	273	337	3rd
1968	7	6	1	.538	303	310	3rd
1969	4	8	2	.333	277	319	4th
1970	10	3	1	.714	352	267	1st
1971	9	5	0	.643	300	216	1st
1972	8	5	1	.607	353	249	1st
1973	5	9	0	.357	262	319	Tied 3rd
1974	6	8	0	.428	226	236	2nd
1975	5	9	0	.357	255	286	2nd
1976	8	6	0	.570	270	190	2nd
1977	5	9	0	.357	220	260	3rd
1978	2	14	0	.125	219	350	4th
1979	2	14	0	.125	308	416	4th
1980	6	10	0	.375	320	415	3rd
1981	13	3	0	.813	357	250	1st
TOTALS	199	223	12	.471	8965	9297	

*Lost Western Conference Playoff to Detroit (31-27)

49ERS' COACHES' OVERALL RECORDS

	W	L	T
Buck Shaw	71	39	4
Nine Seasons (1946-54)			
Red Strader	4	8	0
One Season (1955)			
Frankie Albert	19	16	1
Three Seasons (1956-58)			
Red Hickey	27	27	1
Four Seasons plus 3 games (1959-63)			
Jack Christiansen	26	38	2
Four Seasons plus 11 games (1963-67)			
Dick Nolan	54	53	5
Eight Seasons (1968-75)			
Monte Clark	8	6	0
One Season (1976)			
Ken Meyer	5	9	0
One Season (1977)			
Pete McCulley	1	8	0
9 games (1978)			
Fred O'Connor	1	6	0
7 games (1978)			
Bill Walsh	21	27	0
Three Seasons (1979-81)			

The best of the 49ers

Year	W	L	T	Pct	PF	PA
1981	13	3	0	.813	357	250
1970	10	3	1	.750	352	267
1953	9	3	0	.750	372	237
1957	8	4	0	.667	287	295
1971	9	5	1	.678	300	216
1951	7	4	1	.625	225	205
1955	7	4	1	.625	216	308
1972	8	5	1	.607	353	249
1952	7	5	0	.583	225	205
1959	7	5	0	.583	255	237
1960	7	5	0	.583	208	205

... on the emotion of the Super Bowl

"I was more excited than nervous. I thought I was going to get sick during the game. It was a little warm, but it was better than playing outside here or in Cincinnati."
—**49er offensive guard John Ayers**

"We were so relaxed all week. We were playing rock and roll music in practice. That's what we did today."
—**49er lineman Walt Downing**

... on winning the Super Bowl

"We didn't want to do anything wrong. The game was in the balance. We felt one more field goal would turn the game in the other direction and it did. We played a great football team today. I think they're the best team in the AFC . . . and the second-best team in football."
—**49er Coach Bill Walsh**

"The feeling of winning this game hasn't really sunk in yet. I have a lot of emotion right now, but I don't think it will hit me until later."
—**49er quarterback Joe Montana**

"We had a lot of people that doubted us all year long. They didn't think we were for real. We had the personnel. We had the coaches. And we came from a 6–10 team last year and now we're world champions. We wanted it badly and we got it. I'm just all choked up about it."
—**49er defensive tackle Archie Reese**

"We done won the world. We done won the world. And is it ever sweet."
—**49er defensive back Carlton Williamson**

ABOUT THE AUTHOR

Leonard Koppett is Executive Sports Editor for *The Peninsula Times Tribune* (daily) and columnist for *The Sporting News* (weekly). A graduate of Columbia University, he spent 6 years with *The New York Herald Tribune,* 9 years with *The New York Post,* and 15 years with *The New York Times* as sports reporter and columnist before moving to Palo Alto, California in 1978. Author of many previous books, from *A Thinking Man's Guide to Baseball* (1967) to *Sports Illusion, Sports Reality* (Houghton-Mifflin, 1981), Mr. Koppett has lectured widely, contributed to various magazines, encyclopedias, and special publications. In addition to his many honors as a sports writer and television commentator, he has taught courses on News Writing, and Sports and Society at Stanford University.